STATE POLITICS
IN THE UNITED STATES

Second Edition

STATE
POLITICS
IN THE
UNITED STATES

Second Edition

Kenneth T. Palmer
University of Maine at Orono

ST. MARTIN'S PRESS • NEW YORK

To Janice

Cover designed by Carlos Madrid and executed by Melissa Tardiff

Library of Congress Catalog Card Number: 76-28129
Copyright © 1977 by St. Martin's Press, Inc.
All Rights Reserved.
Manufactured in the United States of America
0987
fedcba
For information, write; St. Martin's Press, Inc.,
175 Fifth Ave, New York, N.Y. 10010

cloth ISBN: 312-75670-4
paper ISBN: 312-75705-0

Preface

The purpose of this second edition, like that of the first, is to provide a brief introduction to the politics of the fifty states. The study of state government and politics is a dynamic field in which research methods are being modified even as the states' own governmental processes are changing. Over the past several years political scientists have produced much new knowledge about state political life, and their work has underscored the growing importance of the states in the conduct of American public affairs. This book presents a systematic survey of contemporary state politics, giving particular emphasis to the states' place in American federalism and to their distinctiveness as political systems.

I have incurred a number of debts in the course of preparing the second edition. I should like to thank Samuel H. Beer of Harvard University, W. P. Collins of Georgia State University, and Phillip E. Present of California State University, Northridge, each of whom provided many useful suggestions for strengthening the book. I am particularly grateful to Richard I. Hofferbert of the State University of New York at Binghamton, who offered important, detailed criticisms of the completed manuscript for the present book. James F. Horan, Eugene A. Mawhinney, and Roy W. Shin, departmental colleagues at the University of Maine, have contributed substantially to my education in state politics in our recent collaborative projects on the affairs of our own state. My students, especially those in our department's advanced courses in state politics and in the federal system, have sharpened my comprehension of the political processes in the states through their questions and their insistence on clarity. I am grateful to two of them, Larry Worden and Charles Bernstein, for providing valuable research assistance. My wife, Janice, typed the manuscript and was involved in every stage of its development. It was her encouragement that enabled me to undertake the project in the first place. It is appropriate, finally, to note that I am, of course, alone responsible for what errors and inadequacies remain in these pages.

Orono, Maine   K.T.P.

Contents

Preface   *v*

   I STATE POLITICS IN PERSPECTIVE   1
     Evaluating the States   2
     The Problem of Visibility   7
     The Problem of the States' Governing Coalitions   12
     An Approach to State Politics   16
     Summary   20

  II THE ENVIRONMENT OF STATE POLITICS   23
     What Is Federalism?   24
     Federalism and the Supreme Court   25
     Federalism and Private Group Politics   31
     Federalism and Public Group Politics   35
     Rural–Urban Tensions   39
     Sectional Tensions   42
     Tensions among Political Cultures   45
     Interstate Differences   49
     Summary   54

 III POLITICAL INPUTS IN THE STATES   58
     Public Opinion in the States   59
     Political Parties   62
     Interparty Competition in the States   63
     Varieties of State Parties   67
     The Problem of Party Responsibility   72
     Interest Groups and State Politics   74
     State Constitutions   80
     Summary   84

IV THE AUTHORITATIVE DECISION-MAKING
    AGENCIES   88
    State Legislatures   88
    The Problem of State Administration   97
    Governors, Legislators, and Bureaucrats   102
    State Courts   107
    Summary   115

 V POLICY OUTPUTS IN THE STATES   119
    Raising and Spending Money   120
    What Determines Policy Differences?   126
    Early Assumptions and Initial Findings   126
    Current Findings: The Mix of Politics and Economics 131
    The States in the Intergovernmental System   139
    Summary   142

Bibliography   145

Index   153

STATE POLITICS
IN THE UNITED STATES

Second Edition

Chapter I

STATE POLITICS IN PERSPECTIVE

Until recent years the academic study of American politics was practically synonymous with the examination of American national institutions. Courses and textbooks labeled "American Government" turned out to be largely, if not exclusively, concerned with events centering in Washington, D. C. Relatively scant attention was given to the politics and policy significance of decisions arrived at in Sacramento, Albany, Harrisburg, Atlanta, Boston, Springfield, Columbus, or Lansing. The political battles in the states remained largely unexplored. Within the past decade or so, however, students of government and citizens alike have become more mindful of the problems and activities of the states.

Several reasons may be cited for this new interest. First, the landmark U. S. Supreme Court decision in 1962, *Baker* v. *Carr*,[1] made state legislatures for the first time a matter of national province and concern. As state after state struggled to satisfy the "one man, one vote" rule in its legislative reapportionment, journalistic and academic writings discussed not only the problems of state legislatures but also the politics of state institutions in general. One far-reaching consequence of reapportionment in the states was that state government was brought into much sharper focus for people who had rarely given state affairs much thought. The new awareness has helped in turn to make the states more responsive to the challenges of the 1970s.

A second reason for the resurgence of interest in state politics derives from a recognition that the states differ from one another in their politics, often dramatically so. There is no single "state political process" that accurately describes all fifty states. Each state has its own traditions and peculiarities, its distinctive ways of doing things, and its particular policy styles. Because such variations exist, a major task of scholarship is to identify and explain their significance. Many political scientists now regard the states as especially fruitful laboratories in which to engage in comparative political research.

Finally, the states are receiving a lot of attention today because the operation of American federalism has become a major national issue. With the emergence of the "New Federalism" under the Nixon and Ford administrations, the federal government has recognized that the resolution of the ills of our urban society demands the extensive, continuous, and responsible participation of state and local governments. Current discussion over the federal revenue sharing program, instituted in 1972 for the benefit of states and localities, reflects disagreement in Congress over the exact amount of discretion that should be accorded subnational governments in the use of federal funds. But unlike the period of the Great Society Congress of 1965 – 1966, when the federal government seemed prepared to bypass state and local units and to manage social programs directly from Washington, the central questions today concern the methods of guaranteeing participation from these governments, not the problem of whether they should be involved in national domestic policy. Because the states are, in the judgment of many observers, the foundation of the federal system, their political viability is essential if America is to make headway in solving its numerous conflicts.

Evaluating the States

The new attention given to the state governments has not always been in admiration. Indeed, part of the current writing on state affairs in newspapers and in popular and scholarly journals has followed a very long-standing U. S. tradition of berating state government. Probably no other political institution in the United States, and certainly no other level of government, has been as persistently criticized as has the American state. "Condemned, berated and harassed," remarks one present-day observer, "state government has served as both the whipping boy and the scapegoat of the American governmental system."[2] Attacks on state government run the gamut from generalized indictments of "backward" state legislatures and "archaic" state constitutions to more specific charges of political skullduggery and corruption. Commentary varies according to the state, of course, but no state government has seemed to escape for very long from the curious "whipping boy and scapegoat" classification.

Criticism of the States. What, traditionally, has been the central attack leveled against the states? The historic complaint seems to be the critics' belief that the states do less for social well-being than do the nation and the cities. The notion that state government is not effectively responding to the needs of society has had adherents in practically every decade, going well back into the nineteenth century. As early as 1886 a leading student of government maintained that "the two natural elements in our system are now the Community and the Nation. . . . The [state] government is now but a sort of middle instance. . . . It is beginning to be regarded as a meddlesome intruder in both spheres."[3] Another political scientist found the picture essentially unchanged several decades later when he wrote in 1928 that "the state . . . is standing upon very slippery ground as a political unit. . . . The nation and the city are vigorous organs, but the state is not."[4] At the beginning of the New Deal an intergovernmental relations expert put the point even more bluntly. He stated: "It is a matter of brutal record. The American state is finished. I do not predict that the states will go, but affirm that they have gone."[5]

The states, of course, not only managed to survive this "obituary," but played a vital role in helping to attain the New Deal's domestic goals. Yet in the post – World War II years, some critics continued to relegate the states to a backwater status. In the mid-1960s, for instance, a writer in the *New Republic* spoke of the states in virtually the same language that earlier observers had used: "The major pillars of the status quo [in the twentieth century] have been the fifty states. Almost invariably, the problems with which the states try to deal call for some combination of national and local effort. The state is merely a superfluous intermediary obstacle."[6] When comments such as these (usually made by political liberals) are added to the stock of slogans of conservative writers, who mourn the "passing of states' rights" and the "march of power to Washington," the condition of the states appears gloomy indeed.

A Shift in Viewpoint? But commentary about the states may be changing. Since about 1970 several writers have found grounds for praise. They have called attention specifically to the reforms that have occurred in many states since reapportionment. As journalist Neal Peirce put it after examining the politics in all fifty states during the early 1970s: "State government has 'opened up' since the mid-fifties. Reapportionments, improved legislatures, executive reorganizations and innovative laws have made state government much more viable than it was two decades ago."[7] In a 1974 article in *Public Interest*, another student of state affairs commented that even some formerly conservative states "have undergone the quiet revolution which has transformed state government . . . into a solid instrument for meeting the complex needs of American society."[8] According to a third observer, "the states show a capacity to handle some of the most controversial issues in society."[9]

Do these comments reflect a basic shift in the way people regard the states? After a century of more or less general censure, can the states expect to be looked upon more positively? It is a bit too early to provide a definite answer. But one thing seems certain. The more favorable notice given the states in the past few years is in large measure a product of the states' rapid growth as governmental units. To be sure, a major development in intergovernmental relations in the twentieth century has been the assumption by the federal government — mainly through grants-in-aid — of supervision of many functions formerly lodged entirely or primarily with the states and with their localities. But the states have steadily sought to expand their own activities and services. This expansion has been particularly noteworthy within the past dozen years. Between 1960 and 1972 the states more than tripled their expenditures (from $22 billion to $72 billion). Their rate of spending increased faster during this period than did the rate for the federal government, which in 1972 was spending about two and a half times more money than in 1960. In the field of public employment, to take another measure, the growth of state governments has been little short of dramatic. In the period from 1960 to 1972 the numbers of state employees nearly doubled (from 1.5 million to 2.9 million). The comparable figures for the federal government for the same period (from 2.4 million to 2.8 million) indicate that the states were expanding their payrolls at a rate roughly six times that of the federal government. By 1972 there were slightly more state than federal employees in the country.[10]

Nor is the activity suggested here simply a result of the federal government's using a carrot and stick to lure the states into new programs that they otherwise would not have undertaken. Some state governments have clearly been laggard in addressing issues, but others have taken advantage of what Justice Oliver Wendell Holmes once called their "insulated laboratories" to develop innovative solutions to pressing problems.[11] Some of these remedies have later served as models for federal legislation. Louisiana has had a system of medical assistance for its elderly citizens since before World War II. Three years before the federal government established a program to finance sewage treatment, New York inaugurated its own statewide program to encourage the building of sewers and sewage treatment plants. In 1965 Massachusetts moved ahead of the federal government with legislation designed to remedy the problem of racial imbalance in public schools.

While the work of individual states is impressive, a significant point is that the states as a group have shown they can respond quickly to certain problems. Sometimes they have helped set a pace for the federal government. During the energy crisis in the winter of 1973 – 1974, for instance, several states granted emergency powers to their governors to cope with the problems while Congress continued to debate the question of providing the president with special powers.[12] Governors in a number of states at that time initiated gasoline-rationing programs involving alternate-day use of filling stations by automobile drivers. To take another example, a total of twenty-three states by early 1975 had enacted some form of no-fault insurance, a plan that enables victims of automobile accidents to receive payments without requiring a determination of fault. Despite several years of debate Congress has not been able to establish a definite course of action in this field. In the area of public administration, before federal administrative agencies concerned with consumer affairs and environmental protection were created, several states had formed agencies of their own in these areas.

To note the activity of the states in the past few years is not to discount the major policy roles of urban and metropolitan governments. Yet a higher rate of growth has been at the state level. In 1902 the states spent about twenty cents for each dollar expended by local governments — cities, counties, school districts, and the like. By the 1920s the states were spending about thirty cents for each dollar disbursed at the local level. Since World War II, the states have generally spent directly between fifty and seventy-five cents for each dollar expended by local government. It should be noted, however, that a sizeable portion of local government revenues comes from state treasuries in the form of transfer payments. In 1971 – 1972, for example, these state payments amounted to 30.5 percent of local government revenues.[13] Thus, in that fiscal year, although the states did not directly spend as much money as their local offspring, they raised approximately $10 billion more from their own sources than localities were able to generate. Figures on public employment indicate a similar rise in state activity as compared with that of local units. While the states nearly doubled their numbers of employees between 1960 and 1972, the growth in local employment — while proceeding at a faster pace than the federal government's rate — was only a bit more than half the increase experienced by the states (from 4.9 million local employees in 1960 to 7.9 million in 1972).

Clearly, whatever merit assertions of the irrelevance of state government may have had in the nineteenth century, they are unsupported by the facts and statistics of governmental activities today. The states are no longer a thin layer of governmental mortar separating the nation and local governments; they are big business. In the light of events of the 1970s, the states might now reply that early reports of their death, as Mark Twain remarked of his, have been greatly exaggerated.

Yet we cannot easily dismiss the long tradition of criticism that has been directed against the states. Some of this persists, albeit in abated form at the present time in recognition of the states' growing responsibilities and enlarging staffs. Some politicians and scholars still believe that the cities and the nation are the truly viable units in the American polity. During the intense controversy in Congress surrounding the question of the renewal of the general revenue sharing program in 1975 and 1976, some members of Congress sought to reduce or eliminate the states' portion of revenue-sharing funds (currently one-third of the money is assigned to state government). Their view was that federal moneys should be directed at communities, especially the larger metropolitan areas, where they believed needs were the greatest. Big-city mayors continue to go to Washington for assistance. Even though the sort of cynical view expressed by one mayor a few years ago ("Everything we've gotten in this city is from the federal government. The state has not done one damned thing for us.")[14] seems to be receding as states address urban problems more fully, tensions remain between many large cities and their state governments.

This chapter examines the states more closely with these questions in mind: What is it about state government, as distinct from national and local governments, that has frequently invited negative assessments? What conditions have made the states especially vulnerable to attack?

One way to handle these questions is to discuss a list of complaints leveled against the state governments and to evaluate them according to the evidence. To an extent this is undertaken in this book. However, the best way to address the matter is to acknowledge that the critics of the states have a point. The states do, after all, differ from the nation and the cities as political systems. But one might argue that the states differ not so much in the vitality of their governments (the historic claim of the critics) as in the way they go about their work and in the kinds of people who traditionally have influenced their decisions. It is important for a student beginning a study of a particular level of U. S.

government or looking at a specific U. S. political institution to acquire a feel for the distinctive problems and politics associated with that governmental level or that institution. The typical city council does not operate in the same fashion as does the U. S. Congress. Local courts differ markedly from the U. S. Supreme Court in their procedures and in the kinds of issues with which they deal. So, one may argue, the special problems of the states should be studied when state governments are compared broadly, as a class, with governments at the local and national levels. In the twentieth century the states seem to have encountered two basic dilemmas that have proved more serious for them than they have for other governments in the federal system. These problems are visibility and a narrowly based governing coalition.

The Problem of Visibility

In its implications for the conduct of state politics, the fundamental handicap of the states seems to be their occupancy of a middle position within the U. S. federal system. The states' middleman role has given rise to a variety of problems broadly associated with the matter of political visibility. Few Americans seem able to perceive, at least on a continuing basis, the specific activities and functions of state government. In a general sense, of course, this problem is shared by the national and local governments. Studies have determined that significant numbers of people in the United States pay virtually no attention to politics and government at any level. In one survey, for example, only 27 percent of the American sample claimed that they "regularly" followed accounts of political and governmental affairs.[15] In a society in which private concerns consume so large a portion of the citizens' time and energies, the problem of visibility is certainly not unique to state government. Political figures in Washington, D. C. and politicians around city hall also often wonder if their constituents are listening.

In any effort to obtain distinctness and exposure, however, state governments seem to bear two burdens. One of these is related to the implementation of public policy. The other is associated with the problem of governmental communications.

The Middle Position of the States. The most serious visibility handicap confronting the states at the present time is associated with the operation of "cooperative" federalism. Since World War II all levels of American government have become involved, on a substantial and continuing basis, in almost all major domestic policies. The grants-in-aid approach, through which a higher level of government (federal or state) transfers funds it has raised to a lower level (state or municipal), has helped to coordinate the efforts of all three levels in grappling with issues such as poverty, welfare, air and water pollution, housing, law enforcement, urban redevelopment, and environmental protection. (The numbers of separate federal aid programs currently total about 600 even though some consolidation has occurred through the use of bloc grants that combine categorical grants.) Despite this interlocking of efforts, it is still fairly easy to distinguish the functions for which the federal government is primarily responsible, and at least some activities for which local governments assume the principal burden. But it is a good deal more difficult to perceive functions especially assigned to the states. State activities loom large in census reports and statistical compendiums, but considerably smaller in their visible impact on the daily life of the average citizen.

A helpful way to illustrate this problem is to ask for each level of government in turn: What would happen if this particular government should suddenly vanish? What effects would the residents living under the authority of the government feel? And how quickly and intensely would they feel them? If we put these questions first to the national government, we can speculate that Americans would feel the effects of its disappearance immediately and severely, especially in the area of national security. Quite apart from its role in domestic policies, the federal government's responsibility for the nation's survival in a world of disputing nation-states is a vital function. Popular discussions of the U. S. presidency — discussions that emphasize the president's power to set in motion a nuclear attack — suggest that the abrupt eclipse of the federal government would be a calamity that Americans would perceive in a matter of minutes, if not seconds.

Somewhat similar, if less dramatic, results would likely obtain were our municipal governments to disappear. Although the functions of the typical city, town, or borough are sometimes regarded as much more pedestrian than those of the federal government, their impact on the daily lives of their residents is nearly as great. Within an hour of the vanishing of a municipal government, we may surmise that a series of major and minor crises would occur to make the urban dweller acutely aware of the catastrophe. Water and electricity would fail, fires would go unextinguished, law breakers would proceed unencumbered, traffic would become paralyzed, and schools would close, to name just a few adversities.

The vanishing-of-government phenomenon appears to work differently with state government. It is easy to point to a variety of functions performed by state government, but it is, at the same time, very difficult to identify specific state programs of which the sudden absence would be quickly detected by large numbers of people. Days, and perhaps longer periods of time, might pass before citizens were entirely aware of the eclipse of the great on-going enterprises of state government — the subsidization of schools, the supervision of health and welfare programs, the building, maintenance, and policing of highways, and so forth. Vital as these functions are for the well-being of the average person, their performance is sometimes scarcely visible in the light of the middle position of the states in the federal structure. Under the grants-in-aid system, every state "spends money it does not raise and raises money it does not itself spend."[16] In fiscal 1974, for example, 27 percent of state general revenues came to the states in the form of federal aids. The states in turn assigned 38 percent of their own budgets to their local governments for actual spending in that fiscal year.[17] The interlacing of state activities with those of national and local programs sometimes makes it difficult even for professionals to draw state operations into focus.

Communication Dilemmas. A second cause for the relatively low visibility of state government involves the communication links between state governments and their citizens. In a sense this factor, like the states' middle position in the federal system, is a problem of structure, but it has a more specific geographical component. In a large number of states, the nerves of state government are located in a small- or medium-sized community, usually in the center of the state, set off from the state's main population areas. The state capital tends to be situated in cities such as Springfield (instead of Chicago), Austin (instead of Houston), Olympia (instead of Seattle), Harrisburg (instead of Philadelphia), and Albany (instead of New York). According to the 1970 census, less than one-third (sixteen) of the states had their seat of government located in their largest city. Historically, the main factor governing the choice of the state capital was transportation. In the days before the automobile and railroad, it was important that the capital be equally accessible to all state citizens.

In modern times, however, the presence of the agencies of state governments in what are often small towns and cities has thrown up barriers to effective communications between state officials and their constituents. A study of South Dakota politics notes that Pierre, the state capital, has traditionally been "thickly insulated by the vastness of the prairie from popular pressures."[18] In some cases newspapers are able to overcome these barriers, but the more general tendency is for the state capital press to reach relatively few citizens. Circulation statistics indicate that capital city newspapers in most large states have a readership that is confined to a small segment of the state's total citizenry. In 1975 Florida had a population of over 7 million, but its capital city paper (the *Tallahassee Democrat*) had a daily readership of only 40,862; in the same year Illinois, with a population of more than 11 million, had a capital city newspaper (the *State Journal-Register*) with a circulation of 55,385.[19] In fact, of the ten largest states, only three (California, Ohio, and Massachusetts) had newspapers in their capitals with circulations of over 100,000 daily readers. The large metropolitan dailies do, of course, cover state news, but this reporting is generally subordinated to affairs in their papers' own cities. Few major papers maintain at the state capital the number of persons that they normally assign to cover metropolitan and national affairs. Such wire services as the Associated Press and United Press International serve as only partial substitutes by operating news bureaus in each state capital. A survey in 1972 suggested that these bureaus are seriously understaffed, with only one or two wire-service reporters working in nearly half the capitals when the legislatures in these states are not in session.[20] According to one report, a consequence of the coverage problem is that presentation of state news tends to be "dull, superficial, preoccupied with scandal, and pitched to the antics of the publicity-minded celebrities."[21]

What are the political consequences of low visibility? For one thing, the average voter's fuzziness about state government probably leads to an excessive degree of cynicism toward state affairs. Muckraking comments that the states are, for example, the "tawdriest, most incompetent, and most stultifying unit of the nation's . . . structure,"[22] appear to have grown in part from the difficulty people encounter in grasping the exact role played by the states in public policy. At a deeper level, the low visibility of the state government makes it difficult for voters to see the connection between the taxes they pay and the public programs for which tax dollars are spent. Prior to most national and big-city elections, a relatively broad range of policy questions receive some discussion. Politicians seeking executive offices at these levels usually quarrel over program alternatives in a number of areas. In contrast, in many gubernatorial campaigns in the past few years, the question of taxes was the central, if not the only, issue. Rival candidates mainly argued not about how public money should be spent at the state level but rather about how it should be raised, or if indeed it should be raised at all. This choice of issue apparently reflected the politicians' beliefs that the average voter felt the impact of state government only in the area of taxation — state services and programs being too inter-meshed with local and federal activities to be clearly perceived.

A Louis Harris poll conducted in 1973 indicated that state politicians have probably gauged voter sentiment correctly in this area. One interesting question addressed to a sample of Americans in the survey was: "If you could sit down and talk to the governor of your state, what two or three things would you like to tell him?"[23] The most common response was simply that "there are too many taxes." In contrast, when the same question was framed to refer to officials of local government, respondents mentioned taxes a distant seventh behind such items as roads, schools, and law enforcement issues. The links between taxing and spending seem to be better understood at the local level.

Current Changes. The problem of governmental visibility in the states has both structural and geographic roots that are not easily upset. The structural situation is probably the least amenable to change. The states began as middlemen in the federal system, and their coordinating role in federal and local programs is likely to remain a critical, if unheralded, responsibility for the distant future. However, the philosophy of the New Federalism, which seeks to assign more powers to the states, may well heighten their visibility. Certain issues, such as land use and protection of the state's environment, also bode well for a gradual healthy increase in the visibility of state governments' part in enhancing the quality of life for their residents. The place of the states in the federal system in the 1970s is a theme returned to at several points in later chapters, particularly in the concluding chapter.

The other component of the visibility problem, the remoteness of state capitals from the major population centers, is a difficulty that the states can overcome partially on their own. Some state governments have taken steps to establish better links of communication with their citizens. In 1972 the West Virginia legislature inaugurated a series of weekly telephone conferences to put the leaders of the house and senate in touch with news representatives around the state to discuss current issues.[24] Initial participants in the program included four television stations, twenty radio stations, fourteen daily newspapers, and thirteen weekly newspapers. In New Jersey, which in 1975 was one of two states (Delaware was the other) without a major commercial television station, the state senate explored the problem of inadequate television coverage. In state senate hearings, officials pointed to governmental visibility as a major dilemma in New Jersey politics and indicated they were encouraging New York City and Philadelphia stations to give more attention to New Jersey affairs.[25]

In addition, citizens in a few of the larger states are finding new means (other than newspapers) through which to acquaint themselves with activities at the statehouse. During the early 1970s three states enjoyed the emergence of monthly magazines devoted entirely to their own affairs — the *California Journal, Empire State Report,* and *Illinois*

Issues. Published privately with some foundation support, these journals analyze issues in their respective states in depth, somewhat after the fashion of the *Congressional Quarterly's* treatment of national politics. In the area of public television, to take another example, New York State residents may follow state activities through a one-hour weekly public television program called "Inside Albany." The program, which began in 1975, opened legislative committee sessions in that state to television cameras for the first time.

These moves do not imply an early solution to the visibility problem in state government. But they do point to gradually improving communications between officials and citizens in some states. As state governments continue to expand their responsibilities, this favorable trend may become more pronounced.

The Problem of the States' Governing Coalition

So far we have been concerned with a general problem that seems to be a greater dilemma for the states than for the national and local governments with whom they share responsibilities in the federal system. A second feature of state politics, one that also sets it off from politics at other levels and gives it a particular flavor, is the role of activists in state politics. The broad point can be put as follows: the governing coalition that has traditionally directed affairs in most states has been more narrowly based than the coalitions that have prevailed in national politics and in most large cities. To speak of governing coalition is to raise some sticky issues. The argument presented here is not that the states are mainly elitist, in that a small upper-class group controls most of the elected officeholders and directs state policy, whereas the nation and the cities have a pluralistic government structure that distributes power among many competing groups.[26] The point being made is less technical and a bit more basic: largely because of the states' problems of visibility, the number of people who pay close attention to state affairs, who feel deeply affected by what state governments do, has tended to be small. Every state, of course, has its "attentive" public, persons who maintain a continuous watch over the state government or at least over certain agencies. But relative to the size of the states' populations this segment has often been insignificant.

The limited constituencies of the states have had serious implications for the conduct of state affairs. We can examine the problem best if we again look at state politics in the perspective of local and national government and politics. Through most of the twentieth century state and local governments have faced a common dilemma.

The formal governmental structures of the states and of most large cities have traditionally been — and in many cases still are — fragmented. Not only is power divided among executive, legislative, and judicial branches, but numerous boards and commissions typically share in the making of policy. Much of this structure owes its origins to the idea, popular in the late eighteenth and early nineteenth centuries, that the legislative branch should be the dominant body and that the executive should be kept weak. As one political scientist has noted, a major consequence of this pattern has been to "discourage the growth of effective and responsible leadership."[27] With a large number of competing power centers and checkpoints, state and local governments often find it difficult to act with dispatch and still conform to their formal legal frameworks.

To their common problem of a fragmented governmental structure, the states and the cities provided different political responses during the first half of the twentieth century. At the risk of some oversimplification, it may be said that the states for the most part attempted to live within their jerry-built structures, whereas the cities developed extralegal political organizations, namely political machines, to satisfy social demands. In the late nineteenth and well into the twentieth centuries, large cities faced major pressures from constituent groups. Immigrant populations needed help in finding jobs, in dealing with the police, and often in securing the bare essentials of food, clothing, and shelter. Businessmen, on the other hand, wanted government contracts, legal favors, and other types of assistance in this period of economic expansion. These differing demands were the raw materials from which politicians and bosses in the cities forged political machines. By virtue of their control of nominations and elections to public office, machines were able to centralize power and carry out policies (such as welfare, patronage, and legal protection) that their supporters demanded. Such coherence of policy was exactly what the formal legal apparatus alone was unable to achieve. Sociologist Robert Merton has described the process of the growth of city machines as follows: "The functional deficiencies of the official structure generate[d] an alternative [unofficial] structure to fulfill existing needs somewhat more effectively."[28]

Only in isolated instances have political machines emerged to direct the affairs of state government. Possibly the best example of a state machine was the Democratic organization led by the late Senator Harry F. Byrd that dominated Virginia politics from the 1920s until well into the 1960s. For shorter periods of time, such bosses as Tom Pendergast in Missouri and Edward Crump in Tennessee dominated the politics of their states, but their power rested mainly on their control over the political machinery of a major city (Kansas City and Memphis, respectively). For the most part, the states, unlike the cities, never really developed informal political organizations to make up for the structural deficiencies of their legal governments. This difference may be associated with the size of the states' active constituencies and with the quantity of demands on the respective governments. The social demands on state governments generally have not been sufficiently persistent and broadly based to give rise to the kinds of machines found in the cities. No irresistible pressures for coherence — leading to vigorous executive leadership — seemed to develop in the states until quite recently. In the cities, bosses and machines gave way to strong mayors (and in some cases city managers) well before World War II, but many states did not address the issue of gubernatorial leadership until the past decade. For the greater part of their histories, the states have been of serious and continuing interest only to small, scattered groups of people.

State Political Activists. It was from these limited "active" constituencies of state government that the governing coalitions emerged to manage state affairs. Although elected and technically subject to broad popular control, these coalitions were often narrow in their scope of interests and ideas, certainly as measured by the states' total electorates. Let us consider two examples. In his *Southern Politics in State and Nation,* V. O. Key, Jr. pursued as a central theme the idea of a very narrow governing coalition in southern states. Key identified one group, white landowners residing in predominantly black counties, as central in shaping the political systems of these states. He wrote:

> The hard core of the political South . . . is made up of those counties and sections of the southern states in which Negroes constitute a substantial proportion of the population. In these areas a real problem of politics, broadly considered, is the maintenance of control by a white minority . . . The black belts make up only a small part of the area of the South and . . . account for an even smaller part of the white population of the South. Yet if the politics of the South revolves around any single theme, it is that of the role of the black belts. Although the whites of the black belts are few in number, their unity and their political skill have enabled them to run a shoestring into decisive power at critical junctures in southern political history.[29]

A second group that has been inordinately powerful in the affairs of state government, especially in some northern states, is one that James Reichley, a contemporary analyst of state politics, has termed "the Squirearchy." A political class composed of "small-town lawyers, businessmen, and country gentlemen" centered in the county seats, the

squirearchy "for at least a century has dominated many state legislatures." What is the basis of the squires' power? For the most part,
Reichley thinks, it is their heavy involvement in state politics compared
with that of other segments of the states' electorates. He notes:

> In many state capitals . . . the Squirearchy has maintained an
> unshakeable power of veto . . . Governors in these states have
> come and gone, popular movements have risen and declined, but
> the Squirearchy has remained . . . Government for them has been
> neither an occasional pastime nor an ideological responsibility, but
> a regular and profitable occupation.[30]

To some extent, of course, the narrowness of the governing
coalition in state government has been deliberately fostered by the
political tactics of its principal members. Historically, the southern
Bourbons have been mainly responsible for keeping blacks outside
political life in the southern states. Until the U. S. Supreme Court
handed down its decision in *Baker* v. *Carr*, the squires and their allies
were generally successful in blocking efforts of cities and suburbs to
reapportion state legislatures. But political skill alone seems an inadequate explanation for the enduring power of such groups in state
politics. In recent history the cities and the nation afford significant
examples of the replacement of one governing coalition — despite its
best efforts — by a new coalition reflecting new interests. In the cities
in the early part of this century, immigrant- and business-based
demands for centralized power and coherent policies helped to displace
middle-class Protestants who had managed urban affairs through a
fractionalized governmental structure. At the national level, a similar set
of demands — favoring the use of government as a social instrument for
improving the nation's living standards — contributed in the 1930s to
the Roosevelt coalition's defeat of the laissez faire Republicans. In some
states, however, the ruling coalition has been more or less in power for a
hundred years.

An explanation for the persistence of narrow governing coalitions
would seem to lie mainly in the failure of groups not represented in
those coalitions in state government to generate sufficient strength on
their own to win a permanent place in state decision making. It is
significant that where changes did begin to occur in the states' governing
classes — particularly in the early 1960s — these alterations were
initially brought about through the action or intervention of the federal
government. Until that time the political processes in many states
seemed highly resistant to modification from within.

Recent Developments. Participation in state affairs now seems to be
broadening. Federal decisions in the areas of legislative apportionment

and voting rights have paved the way for a rise in the involvement of new groups in the decisions of state governments. In terms of urban areas, perhaps no state has been more affected by reapportionment than Florida. Until the late 1960s, under an archaic apportionment scheme, the five most populous counties in Florida, which accounted for more than half the state's population, had only 14 percent of the seats in the state senate.[31] The Florida legislature was controlled by the so-called Pork Chop Gang, a small, tightly knit group of rural legislators from the central and northern parts of the state. After court-ordered reapportionment in 1967 Florida's government underwent fundamental reform. With greatly increased urban representation, the state adopted a new constitution, streamlined its legislative and executive branches, and by 1971 had its first house speaker from Dade County, in which the city of Miami is located.

Other population groups that for years were almost never represented in the higher government offices of their states have similarly begun to participate successfully in state affairs. The 1974 election results illustrate this phenomenon. In that year thirty new black legislators were elected to the state houses of representatives of the eleven southern states.[32] In the gubernatorial races a Mexican – American (Raul Castro) won in Arizona, a Spanish – American (Jerry Apodaca) was elected in New Mexico, and a Japanese – American (George Aiyoski) attained the governorship of Hawaii. Also in 1974, a total of 31 women won statewide offices, including the governorship of Connecticut (Ella Grasso) and the Supreme Court chief justiceship of North Carolina (Susie Sharp). Minority groups remain underrepresented in state government, but a movement toward a more cosmopolitan state politics seems to be underway. As the Advisory Commission on Intergovernmental Relations noted in a recent report, the states have finally "awakened from their long sleep."[33] A central concern in this book is the examination of the changing politics and practices of the states, and of the new groups entering state politics, so that the states' place in the federal system during the remainder of the decade may be assessed.

An Approach to State Politics

This chapter began with the view that persistent criticism leveled against state governments impels us to look for ways in which state politics differ from local and national politics. We have been concerned from the outset with some of the distinguishing features of state politics. The lack of visibility and the narrowly based governing coalition are two such characteristics. The chapters that follow will continue to make reference to national and local governments as the states are examined more closely. It is necessary, however, to compare the states with one another. It does no violence to the argument that the states as a group share certain traits to maintain that they also reveal some basic differences. All states occupy a common place within the federal system, for instance, but they vary widely in traditions, culture, party systems, and public policies. Some states have coped better than others with the dilemmas of visibility and of providing their governments with broadly based support. The next four chapters will take a comparative look at the states in order to identify common political patterns as well as some unique features reflected in individual states. The approach used in these chapters should be made explicit here.

The main concerns of this book are to examine and explain state political phenomena, not to set forth how the states ideally should work. In a word, the orientation is analytic, not prescriptive. But this empirical approach does not preclude the making of normative judgments. Certainly no one can discuss politics for very long without becoming involved in some questions of value (indeed, the very selection of materials in this volume represents certain value choices). And in an area as controversial and important to U. S. politics as the performance of our states, normative judgments seem entirely warranted. But the central task will be to provide a basis for understanding and evaluating state politics.

Some tools are needed to organize the materials of state politics. The fifty states have a range of activities so broad that limiting ourselves to dimensions that seem most politically important or relevant is an obvious necessity. The best way to start is to define the term "politics." Since World War II, political scientists have generally associated politics with the idea of power. As one leading scholar, Harold Lasswell, has put it: "Political science, as an empirical discipline, is the study of the shaping and sharing of power."[34] A focus on power relationships in the study of the states has several advantages. First, it reminds us that politics always involves people and that we are treating certain relationships among people (power relationships) as a central unit of analysis. Such terms as "state" and "government" imply power relationships that have been made legitimate over time. Second, a stress on power helps us to look beyond the formal or constitutional institutions of state governments and into the underlying political processes that shape them. For instance, an interest in the ways in which power is accumulated, used, and controlled in state politics leads us to consider political party and pressure group patterns as well as state legislatures and executives.

The organizing framework of this volume follows the now widely accepted concept of political system developed by David Easton. In Easton's view, political analysis should be centrally concerned with "how authoritative decisions are made and executed for a society."[35] The power relationships that are most crucial for emphasis and study are those that go into the making of these "authoritative decisions" or policies. Obviously, a specific public policy that a state adopts is the end result of a complex interplay of people, events, and institutions. To make these political activities as meaningful as possible, Easton suggests that we can conceive of them as constituting a *political system*. When we view political life as "a system of interrelated activities,"[36] we are concerned with identifying and ordering all those activities — involving power relationships — that influence the way in which authoritative decisions are made and carried out.

Easton conceives of the political system as having several features. First, it is immersed in an environment from which it is conceptually distinct but by which it is strongly influenced. In the case of state political systems, the environment would comprise such factors as the federal system, the U. S. Constitution, and a variety of social, cultural, and religious experiences that help to shape people's political actions toward one another and toward their state governments.

As Figure 1 shows, the political system as such is made up of three distinct yet interrelated parts: inputs, decision-making agencies, and outputs (policies). Inputs grow out of the raw materials of politics — the needs and demands that lead citizens to seek certain kinds of authoritative allocations from the political system. In the case of the states, inputs are formulated and pressed on decision-making agencies by such organizations as political parties and pressure groups. Decision-making

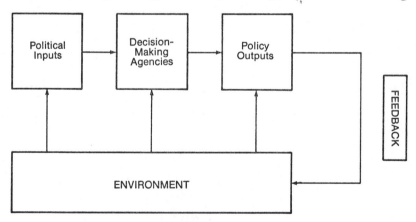

Figure 1.   THE STATE POLITICAL SYSTEM

agencies respond to these demands by devising rules that try to settle the conflicts that gave rise to the demands. Finally, the outputs are the authoritative rules themselves. They consist of the statutes, orders, decrees, and decisions that identify the "winners" and "losers" among the persons making demands. Outputs sometimes substantially alter the environments of the political system and in so doing provide a basis for new inputs. In any viable political system, the feedback process is crucial.

The Use of the Systems Model. Some scholars, we should note, object to the use of the systems model in studying state affairs. Their complaints generally center around important differences between the states and the nation when both are conceived of as political systems. Douglas Rose of Tulane University, for example, argues that because of the federal government's power the "states do not control the host of factors which they would have to control to be political systems."[37] He refers to factors such as the control of state borders, commerce in the states (which is today mainly interstate commerce), and the states' own political arrangements, which elements are all heavily influenced by national decisions. However, one can agree with Professor Rose that national forces loom large in state affairs without necessarily accepting his conclusion that "the states cannot usefully be viewed as political systems."[38]

The fifty states, like all subnational governments in the United States, are much more affected by external forces than is the national government. Employment of the systems model in looking at the states does not imply that we think the states are, or can be, little nations inside a much larger nation. The states are more open-ended as polities than the American nation and other sovereign nations in the world community. The choice of the systems model in examining them rests solely on its demonstrated value in contributing to understanding. We are interested in looking at the interaction of political elements within individual states, and in comparing the states with one another. The approach selected helps in both areas.

The concept of the political system is an intricate one, and its detailed application to the study of the American states is hindered by a shortage of information in some key areas of state political life. Yet the idea of political system can serve as a useful organizing device for integrating and interpreting much of what we do know. Some scholars are presently interested in comparing various public policies and programs in the states, with the goal of determining the relative importance of different political elements (parties, legislative activities, and so on) in shaping the content of such programs. The political system model can be useful in interpreting these technical findings, which are usually stated in statistical language. At the same time, the model is flexible enough to provide a framework for descriptive and case-study materials that illuminate basic power relationships in individual states. The criterion for selecting any material in this volume — whatever its perspective or level of generality — was always how well it helps us to understand the decisions and policies that the states make for their citizens.

The basic features of the political system — environment, inputs, decision-making agencies, outputs — will guide this discussion of present-day state politics. Chapter 2 — dealing with the environment of state politics — considers the impact of federalism on state political systems. It is especially concerned with determining how the federal structure shapes the social and political demands on the states. It also attempts to identify the differing social and cultural environments in which state political systems exist. Chapter 3 focuses on the process by which demands are organized and articulated in the states. A main concern is the different patterns of party and pressure-group systems that operate in the states. Chapter 4 looks at the decision-making agencies themselves. A central question considered is the extent to which these agencies are equipped, politically and structurally, to process the demands made against them. Finally, chapter 5 examines the end products of state politics: public policies, decisions, and rules. This chapter will examine the factors that seem to determine why state public policies vary.

Summary

This chapter has identified a paradox that confronts anyone who seeks to understand the politics of the fifty states. Despite significant and steadily expanding responsibilities within the federal system, the states have long been the subject of much negative commentary. This irony seems to derive from the two dilemmas that have historically afflicted the states as the governmental middlemen in the United States: difficulty on the part of their citizens in perceiving state functions and policies, and the narrowness of the states' traditional governing coalitions. Despite the persistence of these two problems, the states in the mid-1970s seem to be making headway in coping with them.

A central concern in exploring the differing politics of the several states is the scheme or framework employed. The concept of the political system appears to be a useful tool for organizing the materials of state politics. The political system idea as applied to the states focuses on four main political dimensions: the states' environments, input agencies, decision-making structures, and policy outputs. These features of state politics form the basis for the remaining chapters of the book. A particular advantage of the political system model is that it stresses the connection between politics and public policy. The problem of public policy in the states is the topic of the last chapter, but it will also guide discussions throughout the volume.

NOTES

1. 369 U.S. 186 (1962).
2. Alan K. Campbell, "Introduction" in Campbell (ed.), *The States and the Urban Crisis*, The American Assembly, Columbia University (Englewood Cliffs, N.J.: Prentice-Hall, 1970), p. 1.
3. John W. Burgess, "The American Commonwealth: Changes in its Relation to the Nation," *Political Science Quarterly*, 1 (March 1886), 9–35.
4. Quoted in Daniel R. Grant, "The Decline of States' Rights and the Rise of State Administration," in Lee S. Greene et al., *The States and the Metropolis* (University, Ala.: University of Alabama Press, 1968), p. 93.
5. Ibid.
6. Christopher Jenks, "Why Bail Out the States?" *New Republic*, 151 (December 12, 1964), 8–9.
7. Neal R. Peirce, interview, *State Legislatures*, June–July 1975, p. 8.
8. Daniel J. Elazar, "The New Federalism: Can the States be Trusted?" *Public Interest*, 35 (Spring 1974), 90.
9. Ira Sharkansky, *The Maligned States: Policy Accomplishments, Problems, and Opportunities* (New York: McGraw-Hill Book Co., 1972), p. 13.
10. U.S. Bureau of the Census, *Statistical Abstract of the United States: 1974* (Washington, D.C., 1974), section 9.
11. *Noble State Bank* v. *Haskell*, 219 U.S. 104 (1910).
12. The National Governors' Conference, *The State of the States: 1974* (Washington, D.C., The National Governors' Conference, 1974), pp. 35-41. The examples in this paragraph are drawn from this report.
13. Advisory Commission on Intergovernmental Relations, *Federal-State-Local Finances: Significant Features of Fiscal Federalism*, 1973–1974 Ed. (Washington, D.C.: Advisory Commission on Intergovernmental Relations, 1974), p. 12.
14. Quoted in Sharkansky, *The Maligned States*, p. 5.
15. Gabriel Almond and Sidney Verba, *The Civic Culture* (Princeton, N.J.: Princeton University Press, 1963), p. 89.
16. V. O. Key, Jr., *American State Politics: An Introduction* (New York: Knopf, 1956), p. 6.
17. *The Book of the States, 1976–77* (Lexington, Ky.: The Council of State Governments, 1976), sections 5 and 6.
18. Alan L. Clem, *Prairie State Politics: Popular Democracy in South Dakota* (Washington, D.C.: Public Affairs Press, 1967), p. 137.
19. The figures are drawn from Leonard Bray, ed., *N. W. Ayer and Son's Directory: Newspaper and Periodicals 1975* (Philadelphia: N. W. Ayer and Son's, 1975).
20. Thomas B. Littlewood, "What's Wrong with Statehouse Coverage?" *Columbia Journalism Review*, 10 (March–April 1972), 41.
21. Thomas B. Littlewood, "The Trials of Statehouse Journalism," *Saturday Review*, 49 (December 10, 1966), 82.
22. Robert A. Allen, ed., *Our Sovereign States* (New York: Vanguard Press, 1949), p. vii.

23. U.S. Senate, Subcommittee on Intergovernmental Relations, *Confidence and Concern: Citizens View American Government* (Washington, D.C., U.S. Government Printing Office, 1973), part 2, pp. 387, 391.
24. Lewis N. McManus, "The West Virginia Legislature's Public Information Program," *State Government*, 45 (Summer 1972), 161–164.
25. *The New York Times*, March 18, 1975, p. 43.
26. For a defense of the pluralist position, see Nelson Polsby, *Community Power and Political Theory* (New Haven: Yale University Press, 1963). A provocative argument in favor of looking at American politics from an elitist perspective is Thomas R. Dye and Harmon Zeigler, *The Irony of Democracy* (Belmont, Calif.: Wadsworth, 1975).
27. Quoted in Robert K. Merton, *Social Theory and Social Structure* (New York: Free Press, 1957), pp. 72–73.
28. Ibid., p. 73.
29. V. O. Key, Jr., *Southern Politics in State and Nation* (New York: Knopf, 1949), pp. 5–6.
30. James Reichley, "The American Squirearchy," *Harper's Magazine*, 232 (February 1966) 98–107.
31. Neal R. Peirce, *The Deep South States of America* (New York: W. W. Norton, 1974), pp. 453–457.
32. *State Government News*, 17 (December 1974), 11.
33. Advisory Commission on Intergovernmental Relations, *Eleventh Annual Report* (Washington, D.C., 1970), p. 12.
34. Harold Lasswell and Abraham Kaplan, *Power and Society* (New Haven: Yale University Press, 1950), p. xiv.
35. David Easton, "An Approach to the Analysis of Political Systems," *World Politics*, 9 (April 1957), 383. See also Easton, *The Political System* (New York: Knopf, 1953), especially ch. 5. For a somewhat similar effort to employ systems analysis in the study of state politics, see Robert E. Crew, Jr., ed., *State Politics* (Belmont, Calif.: Wadsworth, 1968).
36. Easton, "An Approach to the Analysis of Political Systems," p. 384.
37. Douglas D. Rose, "National and Local Forces in State Politics; The Implications of Multi-Level Policy Analysis," *American Political Science Review*, 67 (December 1973), 1,171. See also the response to Rose's argument by Thomas R. Dye, "Communications," *American Political Science Review*, 68 (September, 1974), 1,264–1,265.
38. Rose, "National and Local Forces in State Politics," p. 1,169.

Chapter II

THE ENVIRONMENT
OF STATE POLITICS

This chapter discusses a topic that is both familiar and complex. As the cross-country traveler who takes the time occasionally to wander from the main highways can readily attest, every state has its unique cultural patterns. In any group of states one finds differences in history and traditions, in natural resources, in the way that people make their living, and in the ethnic, religious, and racial composition of their residents. All these elements can affect the political life of the states. The complex problem is to sort out the environmental elements that are most directly related to state politics, and to understand how they are related.

The discussion here is divided into two general parts. The first part examines the impact of federalism on the states. The single most important environmental factor shared by the states is their common position within the federal system. The second part of the discussion considers the social and sectional tensions within the states themselves that help to shape their politics. Significant data concerning the political environments of the states are now becoming available, and these exploratory findings will be given special emphasis.

What Is Federalism?

Federalism may be defined as a type of government in which the tasks of governing are constitutionally divided between a central or national government and the regional units or states. Although Americans tend to consider federalism a uniquely American form of government, more than half the land area in the world is governed by some type of federal structure; the Soviet Union, India, West Germany, Canada, Brazil, and Mexico, for example, all have federal systems. Federalism is not hard to talk about in the abstract, but it is another matter to pin down the exact power relationships that exist within a particular federal system. In the United States, federalism has been the subject of extended debate that has sometimes flared into physical combat; more than one-half million Americans died during the Civil War trying to settle questions having largely to do with the respective powers of the states and of the national government. Americans never have seemed to agree on what federalism includes in practice, that is, the power and activities that "properly" belong to each level of government. Why is this so?

There seems to be general scholarly agreement that the framers of the U. S. Constitution shared no common view of the federal system that they created. All the delegates who gathered at Philadelphia in the summer of 1787 came prepared to modify in some way the existing Articles of Confederation, but none of them wanted specifically to create a federal system. Some delegates sought to centralize power in the hands of the national government; others wanted to protect the states from the threat of such a government. Moreover, even though a federal structure emerged from their deliberations, the issue of federalism as such never really occupied the center stage. The great controversies of the Constitutional Convention centered around the construction of the three branches of the national government, especially Congress, not around the issue of nation-state relationships. As a result, according to Richard Leach,

> the Constitution emerged with no real clues as to . . . how they [the framers] expected the federal system to work in practice. . . . While there is no doubt that the framers visualized two levels of government, each exercising power over the nation's affairs at the same time, they failed to make clear what should be the precise relationship between them.[1]

One reason, then, for long-standing disagreement among Americans over the specific meaning of federalism is the absence of any clear intent on the part of the framers. A second, and more important, reason is that since 1789 the federal system itself has been in a constant state of flux. Any thoughtful observer can attest that the federal system today in its operations is a drastically revised model of the one put in motion by the delegates in Philadelphia. There have, of course, been certain continuities. A good deal of intergovernmental cooperation involving shared functions and responsibilities has always characterized U. S. federalism. During the 1960s Morton Grodzins and his students at the University of Chicago propounded a major thesis in this connection. The "sharing thesis" held that "there has . . . never been a time when federal, state, and local functions were separate and distinct."[2] Proponents of this interpretation of federalism have called attention to the system of land grants in the nineteenth century by which the national government subsidized such state programs as higher education, the construction and improvement of roads, canals, and railroads, the reclamation of desert and swamp lands, and veterans' welfare.

Yet a larger point is that the power distribution in the United States clearly has changed over the past two centuries. One may acknowledge that the national government and the states have cooperated in the field of public education since before the Civil War. This, however, seems of less significance than the extent of the federal government's power vis-à-vis the states today as compared to its power in the last century. The federal government's involvement in the 1970s in such areas as research contracts, loans and scholarships, and support for libraries and special services makes the federal impact on education vastly greater now than in the nineteenth century.[3] This dynamic quality of the power relations in U. S. federalism complicates the search for an acceptable definition of its operations. This dynamism also has contributed to the emergence of various theories of U. S. federalism, each purporting to explain the "correct" distribution of power between the nation and the states.

Federalism and the Supreme Court

Before looking at two principal theories of federalism, we should note that a critical question concerning any federal system is that of who is empowered to resolve conflicts between the member parts. Inasmuch as tension between the central and the state governments is built into the federal arrangement, the agency possessing the authority to settle these issues is a crucial one. In the United States, the ultimate umpire is, of course, the people. Through the electoral process, and through the power to amend the Constitution, Americans may decide the outcome of issues involving nation-state relations. But in our history the electorate's direct participation has occurred infrequently. Instead, the year-by-year umpire of the federal system has generally been the U. S. Supreme Court. Thus it is appropriate to look at competing theories of federalism from the standpoint of the Supreme Court's work.

The Nationalist Position. One position, which may be termed the "nationalist" view of federalism, emerged immediately after the Constitutional Convention of 1787 and had such spokesmen as Alexander Hamilton and John Marshall. In the nationalist view, the Constitution evolved directly from the people; although the states sent delegates to draft the actual document, it was ratified and put into effect by conventions of the people. According to the nationalist interpretation, the national government is an agent of the people and is empowered under the Constitution to carry out all the objectives set forth in the Preamble. Because each represents only a portion of the American people, the states cannot limit the powers of the national government. The national government derives its power from the people as a whole and is limited only by the expressed language of the Constitution.

Under Chief Justice John Marshall (1801 – 1835), the nationalist position was firmly embodied in a series of landmark cases in constitutional law. First, the Court early established for itself the right to hand down authoritative interpretations of the Constitution, interpretations binding on the other branches of government. In *Marbury* v. *Madison* (1803),[4] Marshall proclaimed for the Court the right to declare acts of Congress unconstitutional, even though the Constitution itself was silent on this major point. In that case, Marshall first held that the Constitution was law, indeed "the fundamental and paramount law of the nation." He then observed that it was "emphatically the province and duty of the judicial department to say what the law is." Third, he noted that the Constitution vested the judicial power of the United States in "one Supreme Court." Tying these three points together, Marshall reasoned that the Supreme Court had the obligation of deciding finally what the Constitution meant — including, of course, the language in it referring to nation-state relations.

Marshall's reasoning in *Marbury* v. *Madison* is not unassailable. He assumed, for instance, that the judicial process was a highly mechanical one in which the only real job of the judges was to lay the statutes of Congress alongside the Constitution to see if they squared with each other. Few people today would maintain that judges can act as truly neutral instruments of the law in this fashion, that they function solely as "discoverers" of the correct law, and that while human biases may enter into legislators' work, they do not intrude into the task of judging. Marshall's opinion was as much a successful political coup as a proclamation of lasting constitutional doctrine. But it helped greatly to transform the Court in the early 1800s from a weak to a powerful tribunal and to lay a foundation for later decisions that affected nation-state relations more substantively.

An important nationalist decision was *Cohens* v. *Virginia* (1821).[5] This case questioned whether the Court had a right of final review of cases initially decided in the state courts, where the state decisions hinged on an interpretation of the federal Constitution or of federal law. Some state courts argued that they could and should determine conclusively the meaning of the Constitution as it affected their own political systems. In rejecting this view, Marshall gave clear expression to the nationalist position. He observed that the United States was now a nation in the societal sense:

> That the United States form, for many, and for most important purposes, a single nation, has not yet been denied. In war, we are one people. In making peace, we are one people. In all commercial regulations, we are one and the same people. . . . America has chosen to be, in many respects, and to many purposes, a nation.[6]

Because the United States was a true Union, Marshall reasoned, there could be only one final interpreter of its Constitution and laws. State claims of power to interpret finally these instruments would lead to as many interpretations as there were states. In that situation, state laws obstructing federal laws might be permitted to stand, and the Constitution and the laws made under it would no longer be — as Article VI insisted they should be — the "supreme law of the land." For the Union to be effective, Marshall believed that limits must be placed on the states:

> The American states, as well as the American people, have believed a close and firm Union to be essential to their liberty and to their happiness. They have been taught by experience that this Union cannot exist without a government for the whole; they have been taught by the same experience that this government . . . must disappoint all their hopes, unless invested with large portions of that sovereignty which belong to independent States.[7]

The single greatest blow Marshall's Court struck for the nationalist position was undoubtedly its decision in the case of *McCulloch* v. *Maryland* (1819).[8] By the middle of the Marshall period (1801 – 1835), the Court had established its role as umpire in issues of nation-state conflict and it had indicated readiness to strike down state activities that obstructed the operation of the Constitution and its laws. The critical question now was the breadth and scope of the powers of the national government, especially the delegated powers of Congress. If the Court were to take a narrow view of the delegated powers in Article I, Congress would be limited in the scope of its policy making, and the states would have many fields open to them. If, on the other hand, the Court were to take a broad view of the delegated powers, Congress could — assuming it chose to do so — set controls in almost any area of social and economic life. In the latter situation, the states might find themselves left with little independent authority. The supremacy clause would ensure that contradictory state statutes would be struck down.

The McCulloch case grew out of a tax levied by the Maryland legislature on bank notes issued by all banks in the state not chartered by the state legislature. The law was aimed directly at the Bank of the United States, a federal entity that was formed in 1791 under Alexander Hamilton's leadership to manage the public credit. By 1819 the bank was unpopular in many quarters, and Maryland was one of several states to pass laws against it. McCulloch, cashier of the bank's Baltimore branch, refused to pay the required tax. The following question was posed to the Court: Could Congress constitutionally establish a national bank to help regulate the national economy, even though none of the delegated powers in Article I specifically authorized Congress to create a national bank? Stating that it could, Marshall used the "necessary and proper" clause of the Constitution (Art. 1, sec. 8, par. 18) to formulate a doctrine of *implied* power. He wrote in part:

> We think the sound construction of the Constitution must allow to the national legislature that discretion, with respect to the means by which the powers it confers are to be carried into execution, which will enable that body to perform the high duties assigned to it, in the manner most beneficial to the people. Let the end be legitimate, let it be within the scope of the Constitution, and all means which are appropriate, which are plainly adapted to that end, which are not prohibited, but consist with the letter and spirit of the Constitution, are constitutional.[9]

The State Rights Position. The Supreme Court's decision in *McCulloch* v. *Maryland* did not go unchallenged. During most of Marshall's tenure on the Court, the nation tended to adhere to a different theory of federalism, namely, the state rights position. This view is associated with such men as Thomas Jefferson, John C. Calhoun, and John Taylor. The year following the McCulloch decision, in fact, John Taylor published his *Construction Construed and Constitutions Vindicated*,[10] one of the most important statements of the state rights position. The essential idea of this view was that the Constitution emanated not from the people of the nation collectively, but from the states. The national government was created to be nothing more than the agent of the states. Because the federal government was an agent, its power should be construed narrowly. As John Taylor put it:

> In the creation of the federal government, the states exercised the highest act of sovereignty, and they may, if they please, repeat the proof of their sovereignty, by its annihilation. But the union possesses no innate sovereignty, like the states; it was not self-constituted, it is conventional, and of course subordinate to the sovereignties by which it was formed.[11]

Under the leadership of Marshall's successor, Chief Justice Roger B. Taney (1836 – 1864), the state rights notion began to find a more congenial reception at the hands of the Court. The Taney Court did not accept the idea that the Union was "subordinate to the sovereignties" of the states, as John Taylor had argued, but it did move away from the stress on national power that had characterized the Marshall era. The Taney Court preferred a doctrine that came to be known as dual federalism. Under this doctrine the nation and the states were regarded as two coequal spheres, each possessing certain governmental powers. Dual federalism held that it was the task of the Supreme Court to keep the two spheres separate, and to prevent the obstruction of one by the other. Judges who adhered to the notion of dual federalism generally maintained that the Tenth Amendment, which says that "the powers not delegated to the United States are reserved to the States," served as a limitation on national power. During the Taney period, dual federalism suited the needs of the nation: it gave the states latitude to experiment with various regulations over the ownership and use of private property. As such, dual federalism was an appropriate legal expression of the politics and philosophy of President Andrew Jackson, who was in office from 1829 to 1837.

After the Civil War, however, dual federalism became a major legal bulwark for proponents of a laissez faire economy. In the period from 1890 to 1937 in particular, the Supreme Court repeatedly used the doctrine to prevent the federal government from instituting new economic and social controls. In *Hammer* v. *Dagenhart* (1918),[12] for instance, the Court struck down a federal law prohibiting the transportation in interstate commerce of goods produced by child labor. The Court maintained that the problem of child labor was a matter reserved to the states and that the interstate commerce power of Congress could not be used to intrude on their province. With the New Deal, the Court repeatedly clashed with the president and Congress by vetoing a number of major statutes that sought to revitalize and reform the national economy.

The Return to the Nationalist Position. The upshot of this was the "constitutional crisis" of 1937, in which the Court rejected dual federalism and returned to the nationalist premises that John Marshall had laid out more than a century before. The Tenth Amendment was no longer to be regarded as a limitation on congressional power. As Justice Harlan Stone expressed it in 1941:

> The amendment states but a truism that all is retained which has not been surrendered. There is nothing in history of its adoption to suggest that it was more than declaratory of the relationship between the national and state governments . . . or that its purpose was other than to allay fears that the new national government might seek to exercise powers not granted, and that the states might not be able to exercise fully their reserved powers.[13]

Since the late 1930s the Court has permitted Congress to expand such delegated powers as the taxing and spending provision and the right to regulate interstate commerce into an effective, if unofficial, federal "police power." For instance, Congress has used its commerce power to regulate activities as diverse as the growing of wheat in a farmer's field, the regulation of labor-management relations in a large steel plant, and the ensuring of the availability of accommodations to blacks in a southern motel. The Civil Rights Act of 1964, perhaps the most far-reaching piece of domestic legislation passed in the 1960s, was enacted under the aegis of the commerce power. As far as the private sector of the economy is concerned, the latitude the Court is prepared to grant Congress in using the commerce power is now so large that "it is hard to imagine what limits there are to . . . federal power under the commerce clause should Congress determine that some aspect of life is commercial and thus regulable."[14]

Given this legal situation, it seems safe to say that Congress, not the Supreme Court, is the focal point for the resolution of most contemporary issues of federalism. The Court retains its basic role of referee for the federal system. It has sought to keep the states from unduly burdening interstate commerce in the exercise of their own police powers. In a 1976 decision, the Court blocked an effort by Congress to bring nearly all state and local government employees under federal minimum wage and maximum hour provisions.[15] And the Court has not hesitated to throw out regulatory acts of Congress that it regards as violating provisions of the Bill of Rights. An example of this is the case of *Marchetti* v. *United States* (1968)[16] in which the Court declared unconstitutional a statute that required gamblers to file federal tax statements and obtain a federal license. The Court noted that such information was being provided to state law enforcement officials in states where gambling was illegal. As a result, the Court concluded that the act forced persons who gambled professionally to testify against themselves, in violation of the Fifth Amendment prohibition against self-incrimination. Generally, however, the Court has acceded, in line with the nationalist position, to the vast extensions that Congress had chosen to make of its delegated powers since the 1930s. The questions of federalism today — whether the federal government should aid the states through a system of grants-in-aid or through general revenue sharing, whether it should by-pass the states and furnish aid directly to large cities or provide funds only to the states themselves — are matters decided primarily in Congress.

This is another way of saying that the real issues of federalism are political, not legal. Although constitutional law is commonly stressed in discussions of nation-state relations, the demise of dual federalism has meant that the states can find very little protection from the Supreme Court for their powers and independence in the governmental system. To the extent that the states have maintained their place in the federal system, to the extent that they have successfully insisted on active participation in national programs and policies, the process has been a political one.

Federalism and Private Group Politics

In looking at the means by which the states protect their role in the partnership of U. S. federalism, we must be careful to recall the basic unit of analysis, namely, power relationships among people. It is easy to make the error of thinking that nation-state conflict is a process in which solid objects collide with one another, something akin to the balls on a billiard table. In fact, the raw materials of nation-state conflict are the differing goals and interests of the 220 million people living within the federal system. Within each of the fifty states there are some people who abide by the nationalist position, that is, who believe in an expanding and increasingly active federal government. And living in the same states there are other people who just as intensely hold by the state rights view, that is, who seek to have new governmental programs established and maintained at the state level. Our federal system currently offers two distinct levels (the state and the national) at which authoritative decisions may be undertaken. Some years ago, David Truman noted that these two levels seem to afford different advantages or access to different groups of people:

> The existence of the federal system itself is a source of unequal advantage in access. Groups that would be rather obscure or weak

under a unitary arrangement may hold advantageous positions in their state governments and will be vigorous in their insistence upon the existing distribution of power between states and nation.[17]

To consider the impact of federalism on the environment of state politics, then, it is necessary to consider those Americans who regard state political systems as preferred levels of decision making. These people may be expected to defend the states' importance in the federal system. Let us look first at some private social and economic groups that tend to espouse the state rights view, and then look at some public or governmental groups that also are supportive of the states.

Among the most vocal defenders of state rights over the past several decades, at least since the 1930s, have been what David Truman has called "defensive" interest groups. In his analysis of interest-group activity in *The Governmental Process*, Truman observed that "a very large proportion of group activity is merely defensive or preventive . . . , dedicated to preventing any change in the existing order of things."[18] Since the New Deal many conservative groups have identified with the states. Segregationist groups in the South have been, of course, a primary example. Unhappy with federal civil rights programs, the segregationists have invoked the cry of state rights to try to maintain their historic control over black citizens in their states. During the 1960s segregationist politicians in Mississippi maintained a semiofficial State Sovereignty Commission for this purpose.

Certain large business groups have also come to the defense of the states. In the early 1950s, for instance, major U. S. oil companies succeeded in persuading Congress to assign jurisdiction over offshore oil deposits ("tidelands oil") to the states of Louisiana, Texas, and California. The issue of whether the national government or the states should properly regulate the exploitation of submerged oil had been contested bitterly for several years. Much of the argument was framed in the constitutional and theoretical language of the state rights view. Yet, as one observer suggested at that time, a more critical factor involved in the dispute was the nature of the economic interests involved:

> The solicitude of the oil companies for states' rights is hardly based on convictions derived from political theory but rather on fears that federal ownership may result in the cancellation or modification of state leases favorable to their interests, their knowledge that they can successfully cope with state oil regulatory agencies, and uncertainty concerning their ability to control a federal agency.[19]

Why have conservative groups often favored the states? One

general answer is that limitations in the states' capacity to act as public regulators may make them attractive to groups in the United States whose goal it is to avoid or at least to minimize direct governmental supervision. In the area of economics, for instance, the states do not possess the kinds of fiscal controls necessary for competent business regulation that are available to the federal government. The states often find themselves in competition with one another to establish a "good business climate" and to win the support of large industries whose payrolls are crucial to the states' own economies. In many states the loss of a steel plant, a textile mill, or an automobile plant is an ever-present threat. In contrast, the national government need not worry about an industry leaving its domain.

Some states also have weaknesses in the area of public administration. The influx of large numbers of well-qualified professional people into government service is essential to the development of broad programs of social control. Smaller states tend to have serious problems in this respect. As Senator Edmund Muskie has observed, "because of antiquated, patronage-oriented personnel systems which hinder the hiring and keeping of good people," state administration is often "lacking in quality and experience, unimaginative, and too subject to negative political and bureaucratic pressures."[20] Americans looking to escape detailed government regulations have sometimes found the states a much more congenial overseer than the federal government.

An additional cause for some conservative groups' affinity for the states is related to the advantages that progressive organizations — those concerned with effecting social reforms — have found in working with the national government. One advantage so far as many reformist groups are concerned is the operation of the electoral college in presidential elections. The key mechanism in the electoral college is the "winner-take-all" rule by which the electoral votes of a state are cast entirely for the presidential candidate obtaining a plurality of its popular votes. The upshot of this rule is to give urban industrial states the balance of power in most presidential elections. These are the states where persons most interested in new directions in public policy — urban dwellers, labor union members, ethnic minorities — reside in greatest numbers. Democratic presidents since Franklin Roosevelt have clearly reflected this base of support in their efforts to establish federal programs aimed at the disadvantaged. Partly to counteract this access, conservatives have tended to stress the limits both of presidential power and of the power of the national government, and to highlight the importance of states.

Liberal groups also tend to focus their efforts on the national government in order to make most efficient use of their resources. Securing a big national victory, as black Americans did in 1964 with the passage of the Civil Rights Act, is usually much less costly, and less time consuming, than trying to win fifty little victories in the states. This does not mean, of course, that reform groups can afford to ignore the states. In order to generate adequate support to win passage of a favorable federal statute, an organization may have to establish some successes in the states. Civil rights groups had won a number of significant legislative battles in northern and western states prior to enactment of the 1964 federal act. Yet in recent decades the advantages to reform groups of using the central government have often been great enough to make it prudent for conservatives to emphasize the limits of national authority and responsibility.

The Variance of Group Strategies over Time. This brief discussion of the activities of private interest groups suggests that the politics of U. S. federalism is, to a large extent, the politics of clashing social and economic interests within U. S. society. The federal and state governments seem to offer differential advantages as private groups pursue their separate goals. Although federalism has always involved a contest for power among groups, the strategies of various interests have changed markedly through history. Since the 1930s, as mentioned, social and economic elites desiring to maintain "the existing order of things" have generally preferred to deal with the states. On the other hand, we find a somewhat different pattern in the earlier periods of U. S. history, for instance, the late 1800s and early 1900s. In these years the states were often the starting points for social reform, for making demands for energetic government, and the federal government was often the reluctant partner in the federal system. A number of midwestern states in the 1870s, for example, adopted "Granger laws" regulating their railroads, but they ran into a Supreme Court veto of these laws on the ground that railroads were part of interstate commerce and therefore subject to regulation only by the federal government. Congress responded by setting up the Interstate Commerce Commission in 1887. Several leading national reformers in the early part of the twentieth century first served as innovative governors of their home states — Theodore Roosevelt in New York, Robert LaFollette in Wisconsin, and Woodrow Wilson in New Jersey. With the advent of the New Deal, social responsibilities that had formerly been lodged with the states were taken over by the federal government, and the latter pushed ahead of the states in opening up new opportunities for middle- and working-class citizens. Conservative groups then began to switch from reliance on the Supreme Court to greater affection for the states.

Certain private groups content with the status quo have in recent decades been important defenders of the states, but their orientation to state politics is primarily tactical: they are likely to proclaim adherence to the doctrine of state rights only so long as they regard the states as more advantageous units of decision making for their particular goals. As the states now proceed to modify their political processes, so, too, may the approach of interest groups change in regard to federalism. In the battle over automobile safety standards, which began in Congress in 1966, automobile manufacturers initially opposed new federal legislation and called for the protection of the rights of the states.[21] When California and New York started to enact safety regulations that were more demanding than those under consideration in Congress, the manufacturers altered their strategy and successfully sought the passage in Congress of federal standards which preempted, that is, made void, state laws in the auto safety field. As more states grow sympathetic to reformist and consumer groups, other industries may choose to center their defensive (minimum regulation) efforts on the federal government. This pattern — should it fully materialize in the federal system — would more nearly approximate the alignment of liberal and conservative forces during the first decade of the twentieth century than the New Deal alignment that has prevailed in the post – World War II years.

Federalism and Public Group Politics

Issues of federalism have long involved competing private interests, but in recent years they have attracted the attention of groups of public officials as well. The past decade has witnessed a rise in power and influence of a number of key groups of state and local officials. Examples are the National Governors' Conference, the U. S. Conference of Mayors, the National League of Cities, the Council of State Governments, the National Legislative Conference (state legislators), the National Association of Counties, and the International City Management Association (city managers). These associations speak for state and local chief executives and legislators. In debates over the manner in which the federal-state-local partnership should be fashioned, these organizations have become major Washington lobbies. They have sought specific federal legislation to aid them in meeting their responsibilities within their various subnational governments.

What common interests link such public officials as governors, big-city mayors, and town and city managers? Both individually and collectively these officers face somewhat different problems, but in terms of the federal system a shared need arises from the generalist role that they all play in their respective governments. Governors, mayors, and managers are charged with the supervision of a state or community, particularly with the formulation and execution of its overall budget. Because of their responsibilities, these officials have become increasingly concerned with the manner in which federal assistance to states and localities is disbursed. Their shared interest is to have federal aid distributed in a fashion that permits much discretion on the part of states and localities as to how such money is to be used.

The Emergence of Federal Revenue Sharing. The lobbying efforts of state and urban officials on behalf of federal revenue sharing is a good example of their involvement in the politics of federalism. Most governors and mayors initially welcomed the new burst of national legislation that occurred in 1965 after the election of President Lyndon B. Johnson and the heavily Democratic Eighty-ninth Congress. In what was perhaps the most productive congressional session since the New Deal, federal programs were established to cope with poverty, urban decay, inadequate transportation, substandard schools, and a host of other problems. These programs required the participation of state and local governments, but they did so in a particular way. Nearly all the new programs were funded according to the traditional grants-in-aid approach, which had been the main device by which federal assistance to states and localities was given since the turn of the twentieth century. Under grants-in-aid, funds are disbursed to subnational governments on a conditional basis. The recipient must follow the regulations of a program to the letter (meaning, for instance, that funds for employing remedial reading teachers for elementary schools must be used only for that purpose), and normally the state or local government is required to match federal program dollars with a certain amount of its own funds (the formulas vary with the individual aid program). Because grants-in-aid programs involve dealings mainly between functional bureaucrats (bureaucrats who specialize in specific policy areas) in the cabinet departments in Washington and their functional bureaucratic counterparts in state and municipal agencies (such as health, welfare, transportation), this pattern of national assistance is sometimes referred to as functional federalism.

As the numbers of categorical aid programs mushroomed in the mid-1960s (between 1962 and 1967, according to one estimate, their number increased from 160 to 379),[22] governors, mayors, and city managers around the country began to resist the spread of functional federalism. They did so for several reasons. In the first place, governors and mayors found they were becoming increasingly dependent on the expertise and "grantsmanship" skills of specialized bureaucrats in their administrations to secure funds from the federal government. Because of the strategic role these specialists played in acquiring federal money, the functional departments in which they worked became, in some cases, quite independent of the state or local chief executive, making it difficult for governors and mayors to coordinate programs and policies in their jurisdictions. In addition, the availability of federal moneys on a matching basis to states and localities led some jurisdictions to skew their budgeting efforts to maximize their receipt of federal dollars. Chief executives found that the hundreds of grants-in-aid programs generally hindered their efforts to focus on the needs of their jurisdictions as they perceived them. Finally, as a political matter, governors and mayors noticed that congressmen and federal agencies generally took credit for new programs in states and communities because Washington controlled funding authorizations. As politicians, most governors and mayors sought that recognition for themselves.

These factors led organizations of public officials in the late 1960s to "take the lead in advocating revenue sharing," according to one authority.[23] Under revenue sharing, federal money is channeled to states and localities largely without strings. State and local generalist officials make the basic spending decisions, not congressional committees or federal agencies. The organizations of subnational officials did not invent the idea of revenue sharing (the concept had been on the congressional agenda for nearly a decade before President Nixon made it a key part of his "New Federalism" during his first year in office), but they were clearly instrumental in its passage. In 1972 Congress enacted the State and Local Fiscal Assistance Act, under which some $30 billion was to be distributed to states and localities (39,000 jurisdictions in all) over a five-year period ending in December 1976. The Fiscal Assistance Act, it should be noted, supplemented established grants-in-aid programs (it did not replace them). However, since 1972 general managers at the subnational level have lobbied to consolidate the grant programs into large categories, through bloc grants and special revenue sharing, which allow state and local executives more discretion in using federal funds. Meantime, federal and state specialized (functional) bureaucrats can generally be expected to defend the federal controls implicit in the grants-in-aid system, the approach under which historically they have preferred to work.

The discussion so far seems to affirm that a "basic political fact of federalism is that it creates separate, self-sustaining centers of power, privilege, and profit which may be sought and defended as desirable in themselves, as means of leverage upon elements in the political structure above and below."[24] The seekers and defenders in the politics of present-day federalism include both private and public interest groups. State power is stressed or minimized in the maneuverings of these groups as they pursue particular goals. But the states also share in the governing of the nation's entire population. To examine more fully the environment of state politics, it is important to consider how American citizens in general regard the states. The very persistence of the states for 182 years within the American polity and the rapid expansion of their activities in recent years suggest the presence of some broadly based popular support for the states that is not immediately related to interest group politics.

Popular Support for the States. A 1966 public opinion survey indicated that the states currently enjoy considerable popularity as political systems. The survey focused on the problem of the "salience" of state politics. Interviewers asked a national sample of 983 persons who had initially indicated some interest in politics in general to state how closely they followed four separate levels of public affairs — international politics, national politics, state politics, and local politics.[25] Each respondent was asked to rank these four kinds of public affairs in the order in which he or she gave them attention. The results showed that 17 percent of the sample followed state politics "most closely." State affairs were placed second by 33 percent. When these two top rankings are combined, state politics emerged in the survey with a visibility equal to that of local politics (50 percent of the sample also ranked local politics first or second, although more people put local affairs first than placed state politics first). State politics had greater visibility than international affairs (36 percent ranked foreign affairs first or second) but less than national affairs (63 percent ranking it first or second). However, in terms of perceived efficiency, the states seem to be better regarded than the national government. In a 1969 Gallup poll, 49 percent indicated that they thought the states spend money more wisely than the federal government. Only 18 percent believed that the federal government was the more prudent spender.[26]

These data suggest that despite the Cassandra-like quality of some journalistic commentary about the condition of the states, people seem to manifest an impressive degree of support for them as political units. In recent years proposals have occasionally been advanced to consolidate the fifty states into much larger regional districts. An example is *Back to Thirteen States*, published in 1972 by economic geologist John Stafford Brown.[27] According to available data on citizen attitudes, such ideas are not apt to receive much serious attention. Americans' attachment to the states as on-going political entities is sizeable.

From what kinds of citizens do the states derive their main support? What types of attitudes toward politics are most prevalent in the states? These problems can be discussed by looking at three significant cleavages in the environments of most states. The cleavages involve rural-urban tensions, sectional tensions, and tensions or conflicts among political cultures.

Rural-Urban Tensions

Back in 1928 H. L. Mencken complained that Maryland was plagued by "barnyard government" because of the inequities of its legislative apportionment system: "The yokels hang on because old apportionments give them unfair advantages. The vote of a malarious peasant on the lower Eastern Shore counts as much as the votes of twelve Baltimoreans. But that can't last. It is not only unjust and undemocratic; it is absurd."[28] Absurd though it might be, the imbalance in representation in the Maryland legislature — and in the legislatures of most other states — continued until finally the Supreme Court held in 1962 that unequal apportionment ran contrary to the equal protection clause of the Fourteenth Amendment. The reapportionment crisis of the 1960s focused immediate attention on the inordinate influence of rural voters on the state legislature, but the impact of the countryside in many states appears to have extended well beyond the state assembly. Two groups long powerful in state politics mentioned in the preceding chapter, the squires and the Bourbons, traditionally have had most of their support in rural regions. To some observers, the laws, decisions, and policies of the states have long reflected "an overdose of the small-town political ideology."[29] Urban areas seem somehow to have lacked that access to the decision-making agencies of the states that rural dwellers have enjoyed.

These impressions are supported by investigations pointing out that rural people often take a greater interest in state politics than do urban dwellers. In the 1966 survey, for instance, there was substantial difference in the "salience" of state politics in rural and in urban areas. Of the people living outside of Standard Metropolitan Statistical Areas (SMSAs — defined as cities of 50,000 or more people plus their environs), 62 percent said that they paid first- or second-most attention to state affairs; in the case of people living in large SMSAs, only 38 percent said that they did. These figures take on special meaning when we note that about two-thirds of the U. S. population now resides in SMSAs. In some states the greater interest in state politics on the part of rural regions has led to their having larger voter turnouts. One scholar found that in the 1940s in southern state elections, "typically from one and one-half to twice as many rural citizens vote, proportionately, as do urbanites."[30] An analysis of Indiana elections from 1934 to 1956, including voting for the office of county prosecutor, found that "although it is not a one-to-one relationship, the general tendency in Indiana is that rural areas produce higher rates of voter participation than urban areas."[31] Research in Iowa politics spanning the years 1948 to 1958 reported there was "a consistently higher mean turnout of voters in small towns than in urban areas of more than 10,000 residents." The study noted that "differences in rates of voter turnout clearly have a major impact on urban-rural conflict within the states."[32]

Rural Areas and State Governments. Why should rural and small-town dwellers generally show more attentiveness to the affairs of their state government than do urban residents? For one thing farmers or small-town citizens are likely to feel the weight of state government much more directly than city dwellers. The roads they use are maintained by the county or state highway department, not the public works department of a city. Law enforcement officials are apt to be state police officers, not officers employed by a municipal police department. The patronage that the state government dispenses to the rural citizen's county may well go to a friend or neighbor or someone of whom he or she has heard. Patronage meted out in a metropolitan center is more likely to be of significance only to the immediate family concerned. Additionally, the rural resident's vote may be personally solicited by candidates running for such offices as state legislator. Candidates for state offices running in urban centers tend to rely somewhat more heavily than do their fellow politicians in the country on local party organizations to draw out the vote. Finally, the daily or weekly newspaper that the rural dweller reads is likely to emphasize state news more fully than a big-city paper. In metropolitan areas the drama of city news may routinely push reports of state affairs off the front page. State governments seem to have their lowest visibility among the residents of the inner wards of big cities. A survey of 319 Detroit residents in 1966 found that only 12 percent mentioned state government first when asked what types of problems they would be most interested in finding out more about — national, state, city, or neighborhood problems.[33] For rural residents, on the other hand, the political world as they experience it may well be highlighted by items of state news.

All these factors support a social attachment between rural and small-town voters and the states that probably goes back well into the eighteenth century. Historian Jackson Turner Main notes that during or shortly after the Revolutionary War, state legislatures ceased to meet at such cities as Savannah, Charleston, Williamsburg, Philadelphia, and New York and moved into the state interiors. He believes "these removals responded not only to western pressures for a more accessible location but to a conviction of the farmers that city folk exercised undue influence on policies."[34] In the state conventions called to ratify the Constitution in 1788 and 1789, the hinterlands furnished much of the opposition to the new federal government and a defense of existing state powers. A century later, the vigorous efforts by the states in the 1880s and 1890s to regulate corporations and railroads and to assist less privileged groups generally — efforts that pushed them well ahead of the federal government in this period — seemed related to the fact that urgings for reform in the late nineteenth century were mainly centered in rural areas. The most reform-minded political party at this time — the Populist party — was primarily a farmer-based organization. Since the New Deal rural areas have tended to be conservative in matters of public policy innovation, and many rural states accordingly have shown less eagerness to tackle new problems than has the federal government.

It would be incorrect to imply that the states either have ignored or can in the future be expected to neglect the issues of urban centers. By 1972 more than two-thirds of the states had set up departments (or offices) of local government affairs, designed explicitly to aid in the settlement of metropolitan issues. The states have shown new interest in helping localities solve problems that affect cities and their surrounding communities such as questions of mass transportation, zoning, and land use. But many states still seem to retain a rural bias or small-town ideology in many policy-making practices — despite their slowly increasing recognition of urban dilemmas and despite the fact that their legislatures have been reapportioned in accordance with the "one man, one vote" rule.

In the decades before *Baker* v. *Carr* (1962), malapportionment in the states seriously handicapped the states' capacity to deal with contemporary social issues. Malapportionment, however, seemed nearly always to be more a consequence of the rural areas' attachment to the state governments than a cause of the problem. An illustration of the persistence of rural influence in one state is found in a study of the 1969 Utah legislature. A group of investigators who examined that institution, which by 1969 had legally apportioned itself in full accordance with Supreme Court decisions, concluded that "psychologically and behaviorally the Utah legislature is still not reapportioned."[35] Their observations led them to conclude that rural representatives in Utah were often more able and more involved in legislative work and drew greater support and attention from their constituents than did urban legislators. In a public opinion survey taken just after the legislative session adjourned, 37 percent of the rural residents in Utah knew the name of their state senator, but only 23 percent of the urban dwellers could identify their senator. The situation in Utah suggests that if the states are to become fully oriented to the concerns of metropolitan areas, it will be necessary for urban voters to match the deeply rooted political awareness and support that rural dwellers have historically given to state governments.

Sectional Tensions

A second environmental problem concerns the extent to which the states may be regarded as political communities. In our early history as a nation, it appeared to many observers that the states, not the nation as such, formed the true political communities on the American landscape. Consider, for instance, Alexis de Tocqueville's remarks on the social cohesiveness of the states during the 1830s:

> The Union is possessed of money and of troops, but the affection and the prejudices of the people are in the bosom of the states. The sovereignty of the Union is an abstract being, which is connected with but few external objects; the sovereignty of the states is hourly perceptible, easily understood, constantly active. . . . The supreme power of the nation only affects a few of the chief interests of society: it represents an immense but remote country, and claims a feeling of patriotism which is vague and ill-defined: but the authority of the states controls every individual citizen at every hour and in all circumstances; it protects his property, his freedom, and his life.[36]

Although it is unlikely that the "legitimacy" of state political systems is arguable in the 1970s, the extent to which the fifty states separately form meaningful communities may be questioned. The involvement of the federal government in many activities formerly handled entirely at the state (or local) level now puts it in a position from which it can "control every individual citizen at every hour," indeed, much more so than de Tocqueville thought that the states did in his day. We have already noted that certain groups of state citizens appear to find the federal government more accessible to their demands; and we have discussed the unequal "salience" that states' affairs have for rural and urban residents. The problem of cohesiveness, of the sense of community within the states, is thus a matter of no small importance to the capacity of the states to effectively resolve contemporary social problems.

Evidence indicates that the states vary widely in the degree to which they can be called genuine communities. All states seem to have on-going conflicts of a sectional nature, either between distinct geographic regions or between their metropolitan centers and the hinterlands. State boundaries, once drawn to embrace "natural" communities of people, now sometimes seem artificial in the light of population mobility and of sprawling metropolitan areas that spread into more than one state:

> A state does not have to have within its boundaries a market center, a metropolitan area, a real capital city, a balance of commercial, industrial and agricultural activity. A state can remain dependent on, more auxiliary to, a market center and perhaps much remotely a metropolitan center, beyond its own borders. Pieces of a state can belong to different neighboring states in all but state politics.[37]

Examples of state sectionalism are legion. Friction has long existed between northern and southern California over such issues as the use of water and legislative apportionment. In recent years, the two sections have manifested distinctive political styles, with northern areas, especially San Francisco, leaning in a liberal direction while southern California provides a base for right-wing politics. Because of its peculiar shape and topography, Idaho reveals a three-way division in which the northern section of the state is closely linked to Washington, the southwestern to adjacent Oregon, and the southeastern portion, where large numbers of Mormons live, to Utah.[38] Florida has historically revealed north-south tensions that led for many years to northern ("Pork Chop Gang") domination of the state legislature through malapportionment and to occasional discussion of secession by south Florida politicians. Reapportionment and the emergence of a new constitution have eased this particular conflict.[39] In Nebraska, on the other hand, intrastate sectionalism (as measured by county voting behavior in presidential elections) appears to have increased during the years 1916 to 1968.[40]

Some long-standing intrastate conflicts seem as lively today as in past years. At the turn of the century that famous Tammany Hall philosopher-politician, George Washington Plunkitt, allowed that his "fondest dream" was the eventual secession of the city of New York from the state of New York: "The feelin' between this city and the hayseeds that make a livin' by plunderin' it," complained Boss Plunkitt, "is every bit as bitter as the feelin' between the North and South before the war."[41] During the administration of Mayor John Lindsay, interest was occasionally expressed in making the city a fifty-first state because of the inability of the city to secure what it regarded as adequate fiscal support from Albany. In 1974 the Barnstable County Selectmen's Association voted to study a proposal for Cape Cod to secede from Massachusetts and form a fifty-first state after the association became embroiled in a financial dispute with the state.[42] Sectionalism within certain states occasionally seems to lead to a low level of public services by their governments. In 1964 one observer noted that while New Jersey ranked seventh in per capita income in the United States, it placed forty-seventh in the nation in its state expenditures for higher education and for public welfare. One underlying cause, he thought, was that "there are really two New Jerseys." The northern region associated itself with New York City, and the southern was linked closely with Philadelphia.[43]

Sectionalism versus Community. Sectionalism is probably a universal dilemma for the states, but there is another side to the coin: all states reveal a sense of local pride or patriotism that seems to overcome, at least partially, the divisiveness of sections. In some states such confidence may be minimal (a writer residing in New Jersey in 1975 opined that his state "had the largest inferiority complex in the Union"),[44] but other states provide a distinct frame of political reference for their citizens. John Gunther in *Inside U. S. A.* identified the notion of state pride ("Maine has great pride. Almost all its people are proud, from the marmoreally entrenched aristocracy of Bar Harbor to the lonely professor living in a shack on a deserted beach"), and thought that it was especially pronounced in Maine, Indiana, Kansas, and Texas.[45] Although "Kansas is two states, or maybe even three," Gunther thought that "no state is prouder of itself than Kansas." The pride of Texans is well known, and politicians have given generous emphasis to it in seeking office in that state. In 1938 Texas elected a former flour salesman, "Pappy" O'Daniel, to the governorship, in part on the popularity of a local song, "Beautiful Texas," that O'Daniel wrote for the state's centennial celebration. The identification of citizens with their state is sometimes enhanced if the people share a set of attitudes that distinguish them from the rest of the nation. In Mississippi, for instance, a Harris survey found that 88 percent of that state's people classified themselves as conservative whereas 64 percent of the national sample and 58 percent of the southern sample regarded themselves as liberal or middle-of-the-road.[46]

In the struggle between the centrifugal pull of geographical sections and the loyalty of the state's citizenry to the state as a civil community there is considerable variation among the fifty states. The variation corresponds roughly to regions of the country. States in the South and West have higher proportions of citizens paying close attention to state matters — have more centralized state governments and less reliance on local governments — than do states in the Midwest and Northeast. In the study of state "salience" mentioned above, 62 percent of the southerners in the survey sample said that they followed state politics "most closely" or "next most closely" among the four levels of public affairs. In contrast only 43 percent of the people living in the Northeast indicated they paid such attention to state affairs. These differences generally emerge from historical patterns of settlement and from such traumatic events as the Civil War.

Even within many of the big-city states of the East and Midwest, however, sectionalism appears to be declining as a source of political conflict. As a state's population becomes more heterogenous, the really divisive issues in politics emerge from socioeconomic differences. Voters divide politically according to status and class, not according to the areas in the state in which they live. A 1963 survey of the members of the fifty state legislatures is illustrative. The study asked assembly-men in each state to name the principal source of conflict in that year in the legislature.[47] In twenty-eight states the main source of contention reported was an issue of policy or ideology — either a question of "more spending versus less spending" or a problem of "business versus labor." The states in this group (such as Pennsylvania, Ohio, and Illinois) included some of the country's largest metropolitan areas. In only thirteen states were the primary bases of conflict reported by legislators to be sectional or regional. Interestingly, these states were mostly smaller, rural dominions where the issues of industrialization and urbanization apparently had not become intense. The largest states do not generally reveal quite as much state pride or "state identity" among their citizens as do smaller states, but the internal issues in the larger states seem to speak more directly to contemporary problems than the geographic conflicts that still highlight the politics of some smaller states.

Tensions among Political Cultures

A final problem concerning the states' political environments involves the different attitudes that people bring to the tasks of politics. Their views of politics shape the conduct of state political systems and give rise to important differences among the states. Possibly the most imaginative attempt to analyze the variety of state political life in terms of certain culture types is the work of Daniel Elazar of Temple University. According to Elazar, political culture is "the particular pattern of orientation to political action in which each political system is embedded." He maintains that the American states reflect three broad political cultures: the individualistic, the moralistic, and the tradition-alistic. Each of these cultures is a special synthesis of rival conceptions of politics that have been present in the United States since colonial days. Elazar writes of these competing political ideas as follows:

In the first, the political order is conceived as a marketplace in which the primary public relationships are products of bargaining among individuals and groups acting out of self-interest. In the second, the political order is conceived to be a commonwealth — a state in which the whole people have an undivided interest — in which the citizens cooperate in an effort to create and maintain the best government in order to implement certain shared moral principles.[48]

Differences among Political Cultures. The individualistic, moralistic, and traditionalistic cultures may each be regarded as having specific attitudes toward political participation, toward the role of the bureaucracy, and toward public policy making in the states.

The individualistic political culture emphasizes the marketplace notion of politics, in which the practice of politics is regarded mostly as a means, among many other means, for self-enrichment. It thus stresses "the centrality of private concerns." Because in this culture most persons will find avenues for advancement in the private economy, those who choose politics will generally be professionals at the business of politics. Political participation is mainly the province of people concerned with the tangible rewards that politics offer. The functions of bureaucracy in an individualistic culture are twofold. First, bureaucracy tries to maintain a free economy to allow for the maximization of individual self-interest. Second, it serves as a reward system for the political professionals. This culture thus tends to support the extensive use of patronage for governmental staffing. Finally, the role of government in the individualistic culture is usually a limited one. Public policies are mostly aimed at serving the needs of specific groups within the population and at preserving the openness of the marketplace. State programs generally reflect a "*quid pro quo* favor system" wherein public officials seek to reward those groups most directly responsible for their own election to office.

In contrast, the moralistic culture stresses the commonwealth conception of politics. Far from being a way to realize personal self-interest, the pursuit of politics is considered "one of the great activities of man in his search for the good society." In the moralistic culture, political issues are community issues and, therefore, every citizen's concern. All members of the electorate are expected to participate in politics. The task of the bureaucracy is "to exercise power for the betterment of the commonwealth." The model bureaucrat in the moralistic culture is a selfless, technically competent administrator whose sole criterion for decisions is the enhancement of the public welfare. The role of government in this culture is likely to be a broad one. Because it serves the entire community — not simply selected groups and professional politicians — the government may undertake extensive innovative programs. There is, of course, wide variation in actual programs: "Government is considered a positive instrument with a responsibility to promote the general welfare, though definitions of what its positive role should be may vary from . . . era to era."

The traditionalistic political culture differs from the first two. The traditionalistic culture "reflects an older, pre-commercial attitude that accepts a substantially hierarchical society." At its core is an elitist conception of politics. Participation in politics is limited to persons who, usually by virtue of family and social relationships, have the wealth, talent, and time to devote to public service. Citizens "who do not have a definite role to play in politics are not expected to be even minimally active." The traditionalistic culture strongly discourages the growth of the public bureaucracy. Bureaucracy inherently tends to disrupt the "fine web of informal interpersonal relationships" at the base of effective governance in a traditionalistic system. Finally, the role of government is, in this culture, markedly conservative. Although public policies are focused on the total community — not on selected groups as in the individualistic culture — the main goal of government is one of the "continued maintenance of the existing social order."

The individualistic, moralistic, and traditionalistic cultures are — according to Elazar — closely associated with the ethnic origins of various population groupings in the United States. Parts of the country are tied much more closely to one political culture than to another because of historic migration and settlement patterns. Elazar thinks that the Puritans first brought the moralistic culture to American shores and that their descendants gradually carried it across much of the northern part of the nation. Thus a band of states extending from Maine to Washington, including all states bordering on Canada (except New York) and the interior states of Iowa, South Dakota, Kansas, Colorado, Utah, Oregon, and California, appear to share the major tenets of the moralistic conception of politics. A second group of immigrants, from Britain and from central and southern Europe, have been the primary "carriers" of the individualistic culture. Most of these settlers initially located in the Middle Atlantic states and in the nineteenth century moved westward into the central United States. The individualistic notion of politics is associated with the states of Massachusetts, Rhode Island, Connecticut, New Jersey, New York, Pennsylvania, Delaware, Maryland, Ohio, Indiana, Illinois, Missouri, Nebraska, Wyoming, Nevada, Alaska, and Hawaii. Finally, the traditionalistic culture is found mostly in the South. Many of the settlers in this region first held to an individualistic conception of politics. With the emergence of a plantation-based agricultural system, however, landed gentry began to monopolize the political process at the expense of small landowners and the masses of slaves. Elazar assigns the eleven states of the Old Confederacy to the traditionalistic culture, as well as the states of West Virginia, Kentucky, Oklahoma, New Mexico, and Arizona.

Application of the Culture Idea. One criticism of the Elazar culture typology is that it is based mainly on one scholar's impression and judgment rather than on empirical measurement. Although much hard data and lengthy research lie at the base of its construction, the procedures used for the classification of states are not known. A further reservation is that the very breadth of the typology conceals critical differences in the style of politics of states allegedly sharing the same kind of culture. Thus, while Elazar believes that the states of the South share a dominant traditionalistic culture, other investigations have pointed to substantial variations among these states. In the late 1940s one scholar commented that Virginia was mostly a "political oligarchy . . . in which political power has been closely held by a small group of leaders who . . . have subverted democratic institutions and deprived most Virginians of a voice in their government."[49] On the other hand, Alabama revealed "a wholesome contempt for authority and a spirit of rebellion akin to that of Populist days."[50] It is clearly not possible to capture all the shades and subtleties of the political environments of the fifty states within a three-way typology.

Still, the Elazar analysis is interesting and has, according to more recent research, held up under various statistical tests. One study has shown, for instance, that states identified with a moralistic culture do have higher rates of voter turnout, larger bureaucracies, and a greater willingness to fund public services than do states where other cultures are thought to be dominant.[51] A survey taken among constitutional convention delegates in seven states found that delegates in New York, Maryland, and Illinois (Elazar's individualistic states) took a more favorable attitude toward government spending and government regulation than politicians in New Mexico, Kentucky, and Arkansas (labeled by Elazar as traditionalistic states).[52] In a third study which examined the degree of support citizens in fourteen states gave their legislatures as institutions, the order of the states was "roughly consistent with Elazar's speculative assignment of states to dominant political cultures." Citizens of California, Iowa, and Minnesota (all moralistic states) regarded their legislatures most favorably, and those of some southern (traditionalistic) states were least supportive of state assemblies.[53]

In other words, the political culture phenomenon — as Elazar describes it — can be treated as a useful environmental variable that explains differences in the politics of categories of states. So far as individual states are concerned, it is likely that in the future most of them will reflect a mixture of the elements of the moralistic and individualistic cultures. In his own work Elazar discovered a blending of these two cultures particularly in the large metropolitan states, even though what he called the dominant culture varied from state to state. As formerly rural states become more urbanized and industrialized, they are likely to produce people who specialize in politics, for whom the practice of politics is a profession, and thus reveal some aspects of the individualistic culture. At the same time, as Americans in general grow more concerned with public policy questions, the tenets of the moralistic culture are apt to grow in favor within the larger states.

Interstate Differences

Our discussion of specific environmental tensions or conflicts in the states has focused mainly on internal differences that seem common to nearly all states. It is helpful at this point to stress that state environments also differ markedly from one another. Every state reveals some rural-urban tension, for instance, but the magnitude of that conflict and its impact on state policy making vary considerably from state to state. In this section we look at three basic points of comparison for the environments of the fifty states. The implications these differences have for state political systems are noted briefly.

One difference relates to the distribution of populations within the states. As Table 1 indicates, states such as California, New Jersey, and Rhode Island have about 90 percent of their populations living in urban areas (defined generally in the U. S. Census as communities of 2,500 or more). In contrast, Vermont, West Virginia, North Dakota, South Dakota, and Mississippi each have less than 45 percent of their citizenries classified as urban. What is called the urban crisis thus means different things in different states. In the larger states, the urban crisis refers mainly to the problem of metropolitan areas. Conflicts that feed into state politics arise from combat between cities and between cities and their surrounding suburbs. In smaller states, a cleavage between the city and the countryside may be central in state politics.

Further, states with large urban populations usually reveal a more structured politics than do rural states. Competitive political parties and established political organizations exist in most urban states to transmit citizen demands to their state governments. In most rural states, the input agencies of state politics tend to be more loosely organized. Rural states may also reveal patterns quite different from that of the national

Table 1

RURAL/URBAN DIVISIONS OF POPULATION BY STATE,
IN THOUSANDS (1970 Census)

	Rural	Urban	Percent Urban
Alabama	1,432	2,012	58.4
Alaska	155	146	48.4
Arizona	362	1,409	79.6
Arkansas	962	961	50.0
California	1,817	18,136	90.9
Colorado	474	1,733	78.5
Connecticut	687	2,345	77.4
Delaware	153	396	72.2
Florida	1,321	5,468	80.5
Georgia	1,822	2,768	60.3
Hawaii	130	639	83.1
Idaho	327	385	54.1
Illinois	1,884	9,230	83.0
Indiana	1,822	3,372	64.9
Iowa	1,208	1,616	57.2
Kansas	762	1,485	66.1
Kentucky	1,535	1,684	52.3
Louisiana	1,235	2,406	66.1
Maine	488	504	50.8
Maryland	918	3,004	76.6
Massachusetts	879	4,810	84.6
Michigan	2,321	6,554	73.8
Minnesota	1,278	2,527	66.4
Mississippi	1,230	987	44.5
Missouri	1,399	3,278	70.1
Montana	324	371	53.4
Nebraska	571	913	61.5
Nevada	93	395	80.9
New Hampshire	322	416	56.4
New Jersey	795	6,373	88.9
New Mexico	307	709	69.8
New York	2,634	15,602	85.6
North Carolina	2,797	2,285	45.0
North Dakota	344	273	44.3
Ohio	2,626	8,026	75.3
Oklahoma	819	1,740	68.0
Oregon	689	1,403	67.1
Pennsylvania	3,363	8,430	71.5
Rhode Island	122	825	87.1
South Carolina	1,358	1,232	47.6

	Rural	Urban	Percent Urban
South Dakota	369	297	44.6
Tennessee	1,618	2,305	58.8
Texas	2,276	8,921	79.7
Utah	208	851	80.4
Vermont	301	143	32.2
Virginia	1,714	2,935	63.1
Washington	933	2,476	72.6
West Virginia	1,065	679	39.0
Wisconsin	1,507	2,910	65.9
Wyoming	131	201	60.5

SOURCE: U. S. Bureau of the Census.

government because their environments contain fewer diverse elements than the national political environment.

A second area of contrast consists of socioeconomic differences. Despite the increasing nationalization of the American economy — and the presence of numerous federal programs aiding the states, especially since the New Deal — individual states reveal important variations in wealth. Mississippi residents in 1972 had a per capita income which was only about half the level of income of citizens in Alaska. As Table 2 shows, the ten highest ranking states in terms of wealth have, on an average, per capita incomes about 50 percent higher than the ten lowest ranking states.

Such differences in wealth obviously bear upon the capacities of states to meet the needs of their citizens. Poorer states tend to pay their public officials less and to have fewer staff facilities for the formulation and implementation of public policies. As chapter 5 will point out, socioeconomic differences in the states significantly affect the states'

Table 2
RANKING OF STATES BY PER CAPITA INCOME IN 1972

State	1972 Per Capita Income
Alaska	$4,873
New Jersey	4,477
Connecticut	4,459
Nevada	4,390
Maryland	4,389
California	4,264
New York	4,248

State	1972 Per Capita Income
Illinois	$4,220
Hawaii	4,187
Massachusetts	4,052
Colorado	4,006
Michigan	3,984
Delaware	3,966
Washington	3.898
Florida	3,885
Virginia	3,883
Oregon	3,840
Wyoming	3,788
Ohio	3,772
Arizona	3,760
Rhode Island	3,752
Pennsylvania	3,711
Indiana	3,702
Kansas	3,681
Wisconsin	3,669
Minnesota	3,666
New Hampshire	3,628
Missouri	3,564
Iowa	3,476
Nebraska	3,441
Montana	3,385
Georgia	3,380
Texas	3,375
Vermont	3,349
Utah	3,341
Oklahoma	3,315
Idaho	3,242
North Carolina	3,196
North Dakota	3,118
Tennessee	3,099
Maine	3,030
Kentucky	3,025
New Mexico	2,992
Alabama	2,963
West Virginia	2,962
South Dakota	2,949
South Carolina	2,925
Louisiana	2,876
Arkansas	2,685
Mississippi	2,497

SOURCE: U. S. Bureau of the Census.

programs with respect to dollars expended in such areas as education, welfare, highways, and health.

A third difference relates to the ethnic and racial composition of the states' populations. Some states reveal a relatively high degree of social homogeneity; others have great ethnic and cultural diversity. Table 3 indicates the numbers of white and black citizens in each state. The data clearly imply that among the several states the incidence of racial controversies has been uneven. Civil rights issues have been at the center of political battles in recent years in the southern states and in many northern industrial states. But the same issues have provoked less contention among politicians in many western states and in rural states outside the South.

States marked by significant ethnic and racial diversity usually differ from states that lack such heterogeneity in the way citizen demands are presented to state decision-making agencies. For instance, states with a great deal of social diversity are more likely to have competitive political parties than are more socially homogeneous states.

Table 3

WHITE AND BLACK POPULATIONS OF THE STATES (1970 CENSUS)

State	White	Black	Other
Alabama	2,533,831	903,467	6,867
Alaska	236,767	8,911	54,704
Arizona	1,604,948	53,344	112,608
Arkansas	1,565,915	352,445	4,935
California	17,761,032	1,400,143	791,959
Colorado	2,112,352	66,411	28,496
Connecticut	2,835,458	181,177	15,074
Delaware	466,459	78,276	3,369
Florida	5,719,343	1,041,651	28,449
Georgia	3,391,242	1,187,149	11,635
Hawaii	298,160	7,573	462,828
Idaho	698,802	2,130	11,184
Illinois	9,600,381	1,425,674	87,921
Indiana	4,820,324	357,464	15,881
Iowa	2,782,762	32,596	9,018
Kansas	2,122,068	106,977	17,533
Kentucky	2,981,766	230,793	6,147
Louisiana	2,541,498	1,086,832	12,976
Maine	985,276	2,800	3,972
Maryland	3,194,888	699,479	28,032
Massachusetts	5,477,624	175,817	35,729
Michigan	7,833,474	991,066	50,543

State	White	Black	Other
Minnesota	3,736,038	34,868	34,065
Mississippi	1,393,283	815,770	7,859
Missouri	4,177,495	480,172	18,834
Montana	663,043	1,995	29,371
Nebraska	1,432,867	39,911	10,715
Nevada	448,177	27,762	12,799
New Hampshire	773,106	2,505	2,070
New Jersey	6,349,908	770,292	47,964
New Mexico	915,815	19,555	80,630
New York	15,834,090	2,168,949	233,928
North Carolina	3,901,767	1,126,478	53,814
North Dakota	599,485	2,494	15,782
Ohio	9,646,997	970,477	34,543
Oklahoma	2,280,362	171,892	106,975
Oregon	2,032,079	26,308	32,998
Pennsylvania	10,737,732	1,016,514	39,663
Rhode Island	914,757	25,338	6,630
South Carolina	1,794,430	789,041	7,045
South Dakota	630,333	1,627	33,547
Tennessee	3,293,930	621,261	8,496
Texas	9,717,128	1,399,005	80,597
Utah	1,031,926	6,617	20,730
Vermont	442,553	761	1,016
Virginia	3,761,514	861,368	25,612
Washington	3,251,055	71,308	86,806
West Virginia	1,673,480	67,342	3,415
Wisconsin	4,258,959	128,224	30,548
Wyoming	323,024	2,568	6,824

SOURCE: U. S. Bureau of the Census.

The next chapter discusses the operation of input agencies such as parties, and how they are connected to different state environments.

Summary

This chapter has explored several dimensions of the states' political environments. One feature is the politics of the federal system. With the demise of the doctrine of dual federalism, the U. S. Supreme Court no longer effectively serves as a constitutional defender of the rights of the states in their contests with national authority. Instead, the states' place in the federal system is protected through the political process. Defenders of the states as political units include certain key interest groups in American politics. Since the New Deal conservative economic interests have often sided with the states in disputes over the appropriate assignment of powers in the federal system. During the 1970s groups of state and local officials, especially generalist officials such as governors and mayors, have sought to increase state power in domestic policy making. Apart from the support of such organized interests, the states generally enjoy favor with important sectors of the U. S. population. Persons living outside central cities and citizens in the southern and western portions of the nation seem especially supportive of the states as political systems.

The environments of all the states are characterized by internal tensions. Three of the most common of these domestic cleavages are divisions along rural-urban, sectional, and cultural lines. In nearly all states, rural dwellers seem more aware than urban residents of state affairs and persistently have sought to influence the policy-making activities of the states. The distinctive geography of the states has also created in many of them divisions based on sectional factors. A third kind of tension is seen in rival political cultures. The moralistic and individualistic cultures, which offer competing definitions of state responsibilities, are especially involved in a struggle for acceptance within the political life of many larger states.

Although they have some similar internal tensions, the environments of the states also differ from one another. State variations in population distribution, wealth, and ethnicity create contrasting bases from which citizens strive to influence the policies of their respective domains. The input agencies used by state electorates to bring about specific governmental action are the next topics for consideration.

NOTES

1. Richard H. Leach, *American Federalism* (New York: W. W. Norton, 1970), pp. 7–8.
2. Morton Grodzins, "The Federal System," in *Goals for Americans* (Englewood Cliffs, N.J.: Prentice-Hall, 1960), pp. 265–282.
3. For a good statement of this argument see Harry N. Scheiber, *The Condition of American Federalism: An Historian's View* (Washington, D.C.: U.S. Senate Subcommittee on Intergovernmental Relations—Committee Print, 1966).
4. 1 Cranch 137 (1803).
5. 6 Wheaton 264 (1821).
6. Ibid.
7. Ibid.
8. 4 Wheaton 316 (1819).
9. Ibid.
10. John Taylor, *Construction Construed and Constitutions Vindicated* (Richmond, 1820).

11. Quoted in Alpheus T. Mason and Richard H. Leach, *In Quest of Freedom* (Englewood Cliffs, N.J.: Prentice-Hall, 1959), p. 224.
12. *Hammer* v. *Dagenhart* et al., 247 U.S. 251 (1918).
13. *U.S.* v. *Darby Lumber Co.*, 312 U.S. 100 (1941).
14. John Vanderzell, ed., *The Supreme Court and American Government* (New York: Thomas Y. Crowell, 1968), p. 98.
15. See *National League of Cities* v. *Usery*, 96 S. Ct. 2465 (1976). The Court argued that "Congress may not exercise [the commerce] power so as to force directly upon the states its choices as to how essential decisions regarding the conduct of integral governmental functions are to be made." This case appeared to mark the first occasion in forty years where the Court struck down an act of Congress on the ground that it constituted an improper use of the commerce clause.
16. *Marchetti* v. *U.S.*, 390 U.S. 39 (1968).
17. David B. Truman, *The Governmental Process* (New York: Knopf, 1951), p. 323.
18. Ibid., p. 353.
19. Robert J. Harris, "States' Rights and Vested Interests," *Journal of Politics*, 15 (November 1953), 467.
20. Quoted in Leach, *American Federalism*, p. 186.
21. Daniel Elazar, *American Federalism: A View from the States*, 2nd ed. (New York: Thomas Y. Crowell and Co., 1972), pp. 215–216.
22. Quoted in Samuel H. Beer, "The Adoption of General Revenue Sharing: A Case Study in Public Sector Politics." Paper delivered at the 1975 Annual Meeting of the American Political Science Association, San Francisco, California, Sept. 2–5, 1975. The estimate is that of David B. Walker. The discussion here relies heavily on Beer's paper.
23. Richard E. Thompson, *Revenue Sharing: A New Era in Federalism* (Washington, D.C.: Revenue Sharing Advisory Service, 1973), p. ix.
24. David B. Truman, "Federalism and the Party System," in A. Macmahon, ed., *Federalism: Mature and Emergent* (New York: Columbia University Press, 1955), p. 123.
25. Kent Jennings and Harmon Zeigler, "The Salience of American State Politics," *American Political Science Review*, 64 (June 1970), 523–535.
26. Deil S. Wright, "The States and Intergovernmental Relations," *Publius*, 1 (Winter 1972), 61.
27. John Stafford Brown, *Back to Thirteen States* (Vantage Press, 1972).
28. Quoted in Daniel R. Grant and H. C. Nixon, *State and Local Government in America* (Boston: Allyn and Bacon, 1968), p. 282.
29. Charles Press and Charles R. Adrian, "Why Our State Governments Are Sick," in C. Press and O. P. Williams, eds., *Democracy in the Fifty States* (Chicago: Rand McNally, 1966), p. 354.
30. V. O. Key, Jr., *Southern Politics in State and Nation* (New York: Knopf, 1949), p. 510.
31. James V. Robinson and William H. Standing, "Some Correlates of Voter Participation: The Case of Indiana," *Journal of Politics*, 22 (February 1960), 105.
32. Harlan Hahn, *Urban-Rural Conflict: The Politics of Change* (Beverly Hills, Calif.: Sage Publications, 1971), p. 177.
33. Harlan Hahn, "Attitudes Toward Federalism and the 'Localism-Cosmopolitanism' Dimension," *Publius*, 4 (Summer 1974), 73.
34. Jackson Turner Main, *The Sovereign States, 1775–1783* (New York: Franklin Watts, Inc. 1973), p. 450.
35. JeDon Emenhiser, ed., *The Dragon on the Hill* (Salt Lake City: University of Utah Press, 1970), p. 212.
36. Alexis deTocqueville, *Democracy in America*, Vol. 2 (London: Longman, Green, 1862), pp. 187–188.
37. Oliver Garceau, "Research in State Politics," in Frank Munger, ed., *American State Politics: Readings for Comparative Analysis* (New York: Thomas Y. Crowell, 1966), p. 4.

38. Boyd A. Martin, "Idaho: The Sectional State," in Frank H. Jonas, ed., *Politics in the American West* (Salt Lake City: University of Utah Press, 1969), pp. 181–200.
39. James Nathan Miller, "How Florida Threw Out the Pork Chop Gang," *National Civic Review*, 60 (July 1971), 80, 366–371.
40. James W. Lindeen, "Intrastate Sectionalism: Nebraska Presidential Election Behavior," *Western Political Quarterly*, 24, (September 1971), 540–548.
41. William L. Riordon, *Plunkitt of Tammany Hall* (New York: Dutton, 1963), p. 65.
42. *The New York Times*, April 14, 1974, p. 21.
43. Bruce Bahrenburg, "New Jersey's Search for Identity," *Harper's Magazine*, 228 (April 1964), 87–94.
44. *The New York Times Magazine*, September 14, 1975, p. 103.
45. John Gunther, *Inside U.S.A.* (New York: Harper and Row, 1951), pp. 290, 296, 498.
46. Samuel C. Patterson, "The Political Cultures of the American States," *Journal of Politics*, 30 (February 1968), 187–209. This paragraph relies heavily on Patterson's article.
47. Wayne L. Francis, *Legislative Issues in the Fifty States: A Comparative Analysis* (Chicago: Rand McNally, 1967), pp. 38–40.
48. Elazar, *American Federalism*, pp. 90–91.
49. Key, *Southern Politics*, p. 19.
50. Ibid., p. 36.
51. Ira Sharkansky, "The Utility of Elazar's Political Cultures: A Research Note," *Polity*, 2 (Fall 1969), 66–83.
52. Sean Kelleher, Jay Goodman, and Elmer Cornwell, "Political Attitudes of Activists in the American States: Some Comparative Data," *Western Political Quarterly*, 26 (March 1973), 168–169.
53. Samuel C. Patterson, John C. Wahlke, and G. R. Boynton, "Dimensions of Support in Legislative Systems," in Allan Kornberg, *Legislatures in Comparative Perspective* (New York: David McKay, 1973), p. 304.

Chapter III

POLITICAL INPUTS
IN THE STATES

By itself the political environment of a state does not make demands on the state's formal governmental institutions. Social and political tensions exist within the environments of states. These tensions or differences form the basis for the expression of varying public concerns. The input agencies that organize those concerns and press them on state institutions — public opinion, political parties, and interest groups — are shaped by a state's environment, and they form a major and a separate segment of state politics. This chapter begins with a short exploration of public opinion in the states, then considers the varieties of state party and interest group patterns, and concludes with a look at a principal target of their efforts, the state constitution. In most states, the state constitution is so imbedded in the political process — in the sense that parties and interest groups try year after year to revise its language and application — that it seems appropriate to examine this instrument after a general discussion of the inputs in state politics. As in the preceding chapter, this chapter will sort out certain differences among the states without losing sight of the total picture.

Public Opinion in the States

The operation of public opinion in a democratic political system has long been something of a puzzle. Ideally, according to most democratic theorists, governments operate effectively when they are able and willing to carry out the expressed wishes of their citizens. As A. H. Birth has written: "No supporter of representative institutions would deny that the reflection of public opinion is one of their most important functions."[1] In the states, as in the national government, politicians presumably try to follow the preferences of their constituents. On the other hand, political scientists have for several decades recognized that as a guide for the making of public policy, public opinion usually works imperfectly. A major reason is that many people simply lack the time and interest to obtain sufficient information to form opinions on political subjects. A survey a few years ago found, for instance, that only 55 percent of the population knew how many U. S. senators their state sent to Washington.[2] Another reason is that preferences on some topics may be held lightly or fleetingly by many people. Decision makers are provided with few clues as to how seriously they should respond to such opinions. Further, modern policy making has become so complex that public opinion is only one of many factors in the formulation of a statute.

This section looks at the extent to which state governments have responded in recent years to the views expressed by their citizens on issues over which states have the power to act. The methods scholars use to determine public opinion in the states should be briefly discussed. Most data on public opinion in the United States are compiled by national polling organizations (such as the American Institute of Public Opinion in Princeton, N. J.) that use scientifically selected national samples of citizens in their surveys. Except during election campaigns, the states themselves generally do not use polling organizations to uncover their own electorates' ideas about public policy. Political scientists have, however, developed methods of converting national survey results to approximate state-by-state opinion preferences.[3] The data discussed here are a product of that type of analysis.

Opinion Research Findings. Most opinion research conducted to date suggests that serious discrepancies exist between opinion preferences and public policies in many states. Professor Frank Munger has examined citizen responses to 116 policy questions which were addressed to national samples of Americans from 1954 to 1967.[4] The questions in these surveys related to issues over which the states had power to act. The policy areas included such issues as the desirability of state lotteries, the need for restricting billboards on state highways, and the appropriateness of state aid to nonpublic schools. Using the techniques noted above, Munger determined from the national poll data the degree of congruence between opinion and policy in each of the fifty states. He was concerned with identifying the number of occasions in which a state had a specific law when a majority of its citizens favored the policy idea, or in which a state did not have a statute when a majority of its population opposed a particular program. The greater the number of such instances, the higher the degree of matching between opinion and policy. Munger found that some 59 percent of the cases he examined revealed agreement between expressed citizen preference in a state and actual state policy. In other words, the states apparently followed the views of their citizens in this period (1954 to 1967) a little more than half the time.

The Munger findings are, of course, limited to the kinds of issues on which polls were taken. But his results reinforce the point made in chapter 1 that the states have long faced problems of visibility and narrow governing coalitions. When relatively few people consistently form and maintain opinions about state issues, and when state decision makers are fairly insulated from their electorates, the correspondence between public opinion and public policy can be expected to be rather modest. If future studies are made on the issues of the 1970s, the current modernizing of state politics might conceivably lead to findings showing a higher degree of congruence between citizens' preferences and state programs. At this point it is appropriate to look more closely at available opinion data and to ask: In what policy areas have states been most responsive to their citizens? What differences exist among the states in terms of their overall responsiveness to citizen opinion?

To address the first question, the states seem most able to translate public preferences into policy on issues that are closely related to their own political environments. As one scholar puts it: "When opinions about public issues are tied to basic sociopolitical values, citizen preferences are stable and intense and more easily identified and acted upon by lawmakers."[5] Of the 116 policy questions mentioned earlier on which polling data are available, the states were most responsive in the areas of civil rights, the unionization of public employees, divorce law, welfare policy, and liquor and gambling issues. To illustrate, a 1963 opinion poll about civil rights found that citizens in thirty-four states favored a law guaranteeing all citizens access to public accomodations without regard to race, while voters in the remaining sixteen states opposed such a statute.[6] State policies at that time closely reflected the preferences of state electorates: thirty-two of the thirty-four states where voters favored an equal accommodation statute in fact had one, and fourteen of the sixteen states where majorities opposed the idea had no such statute. Similarly, a 1966 poll found that state populations differed over whether divorce should be permitted on the grounds of nonsupport. Majorities in thirty-six states favored the idea; citizens in the other states did not. In about two-thirds of the states, the particular policy of the state matched the preference expressed by its voters. State politicians seem able to ascertain with considerable accuracy public sentiment on "morality" issues associated with their constituents' long-standing traditions or life-styles.

Cultural and environmental elements of state politics also help explain variations among the states in their degree of overall responsiveness to citizen opinion. For the period from 1954 to 1967, Idaho and New York showed the highest degree of congruence between opinion and policy, while Maryland ranked lowest in opinion-policy congruence.[7] One interesting characteristic that Idaho and New York have in common is that their respective populations each tend to be ideologically uniform. Idaho is predominantly conservative. New Yorkers generally classify themselves as liberals in national surveys. On the other hand, Maryland's electorate during the 1960s was just about evenly divided between liberals and conservatives, a condition that probably heightened uncertainty on the part of Maryland legislators as they tried to gauge voter preferences. The notion that a shared state-wide value system aids in matching state policies to public opinion is supported by other evidence. For instance, states in which most citizens read in-state newspapers and where most college-age persons use in-state higher educational facilities generally reveal a higher degree of congruence between opinion and policy than states without such characteristics.

But as we suggested earlier, there exist a number of policy areas where the states seem to pay little attention to citizen opinion. Studies indicate that the gulf between population preferences and state policies is unusually wide in such fields as election laws, motor vehicle regulations, labor-management relations, and firearms control.[8] Why should this be the case? On a few topics — certain motor vehicle questions, perhaps — we may surmise that public opinion is barely above the level of indifference, and so state legislators find little need to address the questions. In the early 1960s, surveys showed that although a majority in every state thought it would be a good idea to require regular physical examinations for all automobile drivers, not one state actually had such a provision.

In other, more significant cases, however, a public issue will affect some voters more intensely and directly than it will others. In such instances, the opinion of the general public usually turns out to have less effect on policy making than the activities of the specific groups whose sentiments have been most aroused. For example, opposition by sportsmen and rifle associations to gun control legislation in the states has been intense. During the 1960s only eight states had provisions requiring persons to obtain police permits before purchasing pistols even though at that time majorities of citizens in all the states favored such laws. When an issue becomes sharply contested in state politics, politicians are strongly inclined to solicit advice from that stratum of persons referred to as "the political elite, the political activists, the leadership echelons, or the influentials."[9] State decision-makers cannot very well engage in a discussion with mass public opinion, but they can and will talk over a problem with individual constituents who are active and knowledgeable in politics. The views of these political activists or elites often become, for a politician, public opinion as the politician understands it. It is important, therefore, to consider next the ways in which this elite stratum in state politics intrudes between mass opinion and public officials. The policy-making activities of most activists take place within the input agencies of political parties and interest groups that we will examine in turn.

Political Parties

Of the agencies that link citizens with their governments in democratic societies, political parties have long been regarded as the most important. In all democracies the overriding purpose of the parties is to nominate and elect candidates to public office through the mobilization of votes. In pursuing this mission parties are mainly responsible for determining how the struggle for power is carried on. The extent to which citizens can use government to satisfy their own needs depends substantially on the operation of the parties. "As a matter of fact," writes one scholar, "the condition of the parties is the best possible evidence of the nature of any regime."[10]

Students of U. S. political parties have long called attention to the deceptive nature of their formal structures. Divided into national, state, county, city, ward, and precinct committees, the organizations of the national Republican and Democratic parties appear to resemble a military force, or perhaps the kind of rigidly structured Prussian bureaucracy described by sociologist Max Weber at the beginning of this century. Yet the facts of political life of U. S. parties are at odds with this appearance. In their account of the operation of the two national party committees — supposedly the commanding units of the parties — Cornelius Cotter and Bernard Hennessy write:

It cannot be too often stressed that political power in America is drastically decentralized, focused in the cities and counties. American politics is feudal in nature. The state committees may have some important power bases in the statutes and state elective offices. The national committees as collective agencies have only that fleeting coalescence of power which comes with the mobilization of presidential campaigns and the integrative influence of an incumbent president.[11]

Decentralization of power is clearly a cardinal feature of U. S. parties. And because power so often devolves on state and local parties, a discussion of state parties should not only illuminate a key dimension of state politics, but also shed light on some aspects of national politics.

The treatment of state parties that follows centers on three general topics. The first is the relative strength of two-party politics in the states. Is our national two-party system built on a roster of one-party states (some mostly Democratic, others mostly Republican) or does it reflect the presence of a large number of states that are two-party themselves? Second, we will examine the various types of one- and two-party systems in the states. Knowing simply that a state has a one- or a two-party system tells us little about the infrastructure of the parties, or about the kind of cement that binds members of the same party. Finally, we are concerned with the problem of party responsibility. To what extent can and do state parties offer meaningful alternatives to state electorates in making public policy? Each of these topics — party competition, varieties of parties, and party responsibility — has been the subject of considerable scholarly research over the past two decades.

Interparty Competition in the States

To even the most casual political observer, presidential elections over the past two decades have brought about a minor revolution in political party affiliations. Prior to the election of Dwight D. Eisenhower in 1952, certain areas of the country seemed to be permanently in the hands of one or the other major party. Democratic candidates at all levels, including presidential contenders, could regularly count on overwhelming support from voters in the eleven states of the Old Confederacy. Republican candidates at all levels normally did almost as well in the northern New England states of Maine, New Hampshire, and Vermont. Region was, in other words, an important factor in the major parties' composition. No matter how devastating a defeat a party might suffer nationally, it could usually count on one region of the country to remain tidily within its grasp.

Since the early 1950s the importance of region to the national parties has declined dramatically. The once "Solid South" has become a competitive battleground in presidential elections. In 1964 Democrat Lyndon Johnson lost Alabama, Georgia, Louisiana, Mississippi, and South Carolina to Republican Barry Goldwater. In the 1968 elections Democrat Hubert Humphrey conceded five southern states to Republican Richard Nixon and five to Independent George Wallace, and carried in the South only the state of Texas. Richard Nixon carried all eleven states of the Old Confederacy in his sweep over George McGovern in 1972. Northern New England has also become much more competitive in presidential contests. Maine, New Hampshire, and Vermont all broke from the Republican ranks in 1964 to support Lyndon Johnson. Maine's apostasy continued into 1968 when it chose Humphrey over Nixon. The kaleidoscopic nature of these presidential election patterns may be summarized in this way: in the five presidential elections from 1956 through 1972, Arizona was the only state in the Union to consistently support the same party.

So far as contests for control of the state government are concerned, on the other hand, the states do not reveal as clear a tendency toward two-partyism. A few states seem quite able to assume a two-party posture in the quadrennial presidential sweepstakes, but maintain an overwhelming attachment to one party in their domestic contests. A good case in point is Texas. If we look only at recent presidential races the Lone Star State appears to be a hotly contested, two-party battleground. The mean Republican vote in presidential elections for the years 1952 through 1972 was 50 percent. Eisenhower carried Texas in both his races; Nixon barely missed winning its electoral votes in 1960 and in 1968, and he carried the state in 1972. On the other hand, elections to the Texas state legislature during the same time period regularly produced huge Democratic majorities. Republicans managed to elect only one member to the state legislature in the 1950s. Their strongest showing in this period was in the 1972 elections, when they secured 3 of the 31 state senate seats and 17 of the 150 state house seats.[12] Presidential voting statistics are not a reliable guide to interparty competition in state politics.

A useful general survey of interparty competition in the states, stressing state elections, was done by Austin Ranney.[13] Ranney ascertained the level of party competition in each state in the early 1970s by using four distinct measures. For the period from 1956 to 1970 he considered: (1) the average percentage of the popular vote won by Democratic gubernatorial candidates, (2) the average percentage of seats in the state senate held by Democrats, (3) the average percentage of seats in the lower house held by Democrats, and (4) the percentage of all terms for governor, state senate, and state house held by Democrats. He then averaged the four percentages. The higher a state's score, the more fully it was committed, at least in electoral behavior, to the Democratic party.

Ranney found that by using a fairly broad definition of two-partyism he could classify twenty-eight states in that category. In these two-party states, Democrats obtained between 35 and 70 percent of the gubernatorial popular votes and legislative seats between 1956 and 1970. Five states that fell between 20 and 35 percent were labeled as modified one-party Republican. Ten states ranked within the 70 to 85 percent range and were called modified one-party Democratic. Finally, seven states fell within the 85 to 100 percent range. These states were classified as one-party Democratic states.

Which states fit in which category? To a considerable extent, these findings on state interparty competition dovetail with the typology of state political cultures discussed in the last chapter. The twenty-eight two-party states comprise all but two of the individualistic states (Massachusetts, Rhode Island, Connecticut, New York, New Jersey, Pennsylvania, Delaware, Ohio, Indiana, Illinois, Nebraska, Wyoming, Nevada, Hawaii, and Alaska), twelve of the larger moralistic states (Maine, Michigan, Wisconsin, Minnesota, Iowa, Colorado, Montana, Utah, Idaho, Washington, Oregon, and California), and one traditionalistic state (Arizona). The seventeen states classified as one-party Democratic or modified one-party Democratic include all the southern states that share a traditionalistic political culture (except Arizona), plus the border states of Maryland and Missouri. (The strictly one-party Democratic states are the states of the Old Confederacy, excepting Virginia, North Carolina, Tennessee, and Florida; the modified one-party Democratic states include these four plus the states of Oklahoma, Kentucky, West Virginia, Maryland, New Mexico, and Missouri). Finally the five modified one-party Republican states consist of relatively small moralistic states mostly in the North (New Hampshire, Vermont, North Dakota, South Dakota, and Kansas). In general, two-party states tend to have an individualistic political culture, and one-party states seem to reflect either a traditionalistic or a moralistic culture, depending on their geographical location.

Apart from political culture two-party states differ from one-party states in terms of certain demographic variables. On the whole, two-party states tend to be more urbanized, to have higher levels of per capita income, and to have larger proportions of their work force engaged in industrial occupations than do one-party or modified one-party states. For instance, in two-party states in the Ranney study, 68 percent of the citizens lived in urban areas, whereas in one-party and modified one-party states, between 46 and 57 percent of their population resided in urban centers.

A *Long-term Growth of Two-partyism.* Because the nation as a whole is becoming more urbanized and industrialized, we may speculate that the incidence of state two-partyism is spreading. To determine what trend exists toward two-partyism it is useful to look at the proportions of seats held by Democrats and Republicans in the lower houses of state legislatures since World War II. If a state is really assuming a two-party model — and, in the judgment of some observers, thus offering their voters some choices in public policy — this pattern should be reflected year by year in the distribution of seats in the lower house of its state assembly.

Using a generous definition of two-partyism — namely, a legislative body in which the minority party has more than one-third of the seats — we find a steady, if gradual, trend toward more and more state legislatures assuming a two-party mold.[14] From 1946 through 1955, 74 (32 percent) of the state lower houses elected during this period (usually at two-year intervals) had minority parties with more than one-third of the total number of seats. In the years 1956 through 1965, 112 (49 percent) of the state houses of representatives had a two-party situation. In the most recent period, 1966 through 1975, 124 (54 percent) of state lower chambers had a competitive situation. Presently, then, about one of every two elections for members of the lower houses of state legislatures finds the minority party with more than one-third of the seats. Arizona, Connecticut, Maine, Ohio, Oregon, Tennessee, Vermont, and Wisconsin all had competitive arrangements only once or not at all during the first period (1946 to 1955), but in at least eight of the ten years of the second period (1966 to 1975). Republicans still have a long way to go in the southern states. They have won more than one-third of the seats consistently in Tennessee since 1966, but in the years 1946 through 1975 the only other southern state showing a sizeable Republican contingent was Florida. The party was competitive in the Florida House of Representatives in the 1969 and 1973 legislative sessions. And a few states — notably, Massachusetts, Missouri, Nevada, and Rhode Island — actually became somewhat less competitive in their lower houses in the 1960s and early 1970s than they had been in earlier periods because of very large Democratic majorities.

The overall pattern has been one of more states becoming competitive in their internal politics, even though their two-partyism in this respect is not nearly as sharply etched as in presidential races. Factors that account for the rise of two-party competition are the growing urbanization of formerly rural states, and an increase in issue-oriented politics in many states. Democratic landslides in the 1974 and 1976 elections have, however, slowed the growth of two-partyism for the present.

Varieties of State Parties

A major characteristic of U. S. national parties is their marked decentralization. Virtually the same description also applies to most state parties: state party organizations have relatively little power, either legally or in practice, over their precinct, ward, and county organizations. Nearly all states go to elaborate length to spell out the legal powers of state and local party units, their manner of election, and so forth. But the effect is generally to segment power, not to concentrate it in the hands of a state central committee. In Illinois, for instance, precinct committee members are chosen by the registered party voters in their precincts for a term of four years; they cannot be removed by the county or state committees even if they work for the opposition party (which some have actually done).[15]

The predominantly rural nature of the states' political environments has reinforced the legal decentralization of state parties. Strong party organizations or "machines" in the United States have flourished principally in large cities. The lower level of interest paid to state politics by urban dwellers as compared to rural citizens has tended to preclude the extension of big-city organizations to state politics as a whole. Rural and small-town residents, who are most attentive to state politics, usually live in areas where local party organizations are the most informal and amorphous. And the habits developed there tend to characterize political life at the state capital.

Yet the states vary significantly in the location of power within their parties, as they do in the extent to which they maintain one- or two-party systems. No detailed survey is possible in this brief volume, but we should note several types of party structures, each of which commonly exists within the states. Differences in structure affect the extent to which the party can offer meaningful public policy alternatives to voters — that is, how well a party, once it takes control of the state government, responds to the needs of citizens in making public policy. In some states, the party system virtually precludes any serious discussion of public interest questions. In other states the parties seem continually able to offer choices of public policy — in their own primaries and in general elections — and to actuate certain programs when they are victorious at the polls.

States with One-party Systems. Let us begin with states that have traditionally clung to one-party systems. Despite the absence of serious competition in general elections, there are differences among one-party states in the operation of the dominant party's primaries. The *multifactional* one-party system seems to be the most primitive form of party arrangement, in that it approximates an outright nonpartisan system. A state with a multifactional one-party system is marked by the near absence of stable blocs of voters and leaders that persist from one election to another. As V. O. Key, Jr., wrote of this pattern in the 1940s with reference to Alabama: "Political factions form and reform. . . . Voters group themselves in one faction and then in another in the most confusing fashion."[16]

How do voters distinguish between factions in this kind of one-party state? They do so mostly according to the personalities of the candidates. Multifactional Democratic parties in southern states have probably produced as colorful a group of politicians as have been seen anywhere on the American landscape: Jim "Pa" and Miriam "Ma" Ferguson of Texas ("Ma" ran successfully for governor in 1924 after "Pa" had been impeached and removed from the governorship by the state legislature), "Kissin' " Jim Folsom of Alabama (who carried his specialty so far that he found himself involved in a paternity suit), and Gene "Wild Man from Sugar Creek" Talmadge of Georgia (who ran in every statewide Democratic party primary save one from 1926 to 1946 and was governor for three terms). Personalities such as these helped to bring the misty world of state government and politics into clear, sometimes appallingly clear, focus for their citizens.

Within a multifactional state, the factions are built entirely around the personalities of the leading contenders for public office. When a politician disappears from the political scene his followers move into the camp of a new leader, who may have little in common politically with the original leader. Consequently, although issues may be discussed in a multifactional state, the factions themselves are too short-lived, and far too amorphous, to implement coherent programs of policy once they are elected to office. Indeed, multifactional systems make fundamental political change almost impossible, and they usually produce a status quo politics highly favorable to elitist groups. During the 1950s and early 1960s, Alabama, Florida, Mississippi, Texas, and Vermont generally had a multifactional pattern in their dominant parties.

A second type of one-party system, somewhat less common today than in past years, is the *dominant faction* arrangement. In one respect this model is the opposite of the multifactional system. The power in the majority party is centralized within a disciplined hierarchy, usually headed by a single forceful leader. In the nineteenth century several states had this pattern. From the Civil War to the early 1920s, the Pennsylvania Republican party had a dominant faction under the successive control of three conservative, probusiness U. S. senators, Simon Cameron (1865 – 1887), Matthew Quay (1887 – 1904), and Boies "Big Grizzly" Penrose (1904 – 1921). These men largely dictated nominations and policies for the state party. During his approximately forty-year political career as Virginia's governor and U. S. senator, Harry F. Byrd managed what is often regarded as the modern prototype of the dominant faction one-party system. Byrd's Democratic machine consisted of about one thousand professional politicians who were bound "tightly to the state leadership . . . in almost all the counties and cities."[17] Despite structural differences with the more fluid and amorphous multifactional pattern, the dominant faction arrangement has much the same effect in its operations in that it, too, offers voters relatively little choice over public policy alternatives. In the post-World War II years South Carolina, Rhode Island, and Virginia revealed a dominant faction alignment much of the time. Virginia politics changed rapidly after the death of Senator Byrd in 1966, however. The once powerful Democratic organization fell into such disarray that it could not offer a candidate in the 1973 gubernatorial election, in which Republican Mills Godwin defeated Independent Henry Howell. On the other hand the 1960s saw Alabama moving from a multifactional to a dominant faction system under the political tutelage of Governor George Wallace.

The only type of one-party system that does provide the electorate with some choice over issues is a bifactional structure. Louisiana for many years revealed perhaps the classic example of one-party bifactionalism. Beginning with Huey Long's first campaigns for governor in the 1920s and continuing well into the 1950s, Democratic primaries in Louisiana were contests between pro-Long and anti-Long candidates.[18] Each faction had a distinct social base in state politics. The core of pro-Long strength lay in Protestant northern Louisiana, especially among low-income farmers and industrial workers. Anti-Long politicians generally spoke for the more prosperous, and more conservative, elements in the state, centered around New Orleans. State legislative candidates would often associate themselves with the leaders of one or the other faction. Thus the Louisiana voter usually had a choice between two distinguishable slates of candidates in the Democratic primary. The slates would typically differ in their approaches to state public spending and governmental management.

Bifactionalism has also been common in recent years in the dominant Democratic parties of Tennessee, New Mexico, North Carolina, and Kentucky, although the pattern has sometimes assumed a form different from the Louisiana model. In Kentucky, for instance, factional conflict in the Democratic party is not between regions of the state or classes of voters. Instead, as specialists in modern Kentucky politics have pointed out, the main difference between Democratic factions in Kentucky is more often simply "between those in power and those who are seeking power."[19]

States with Two-party Arrangements. Much as one-party systems in the states vary greatly in the ways in which they accumulate power and respond to the concerns of citizens, so do two-party systems differ. A two-party system potentially affords a basis for offering public policy alternatives to voters, but it accomplishes this with uneven success. The *personality-oriented* two-party arrangement usually fails to offer much meaningful choice to the electorate. In this system the strength of the parties ebbs and flows depending on the degree of charisma and appeal of the party leaders and candidates. California has been a leading example of this kind of two-party politics in the postwar period. Despite a substantial advantage in party registration, California Democrats lost five of the eight gubernatorial races from 1946 through 1974. Republican successes were due in great part to their ability to nominate magnetic candidates, notably, Earl Warren and Ronald Reagan, and to their more skillful use of the mass media. Voting in the California legislature has not generally followed party lines, for public policy has typically been produced by shifting coalitions that are nearly impossible for voters to hold accountable.[20]

A personality-oriented system seems to be especially characteristic of a state at the time when it is moving from a one-party into a two-party pattern. In Maine in the mid-1960s, for example, the Democratic party became for the first time entirely competitive with Republicans in statewide contests. Maine Democrats achieved this success by concentrating their talents and resources on major offices and by emphasizing the personality and style of their candidates, particularly Senator Edmund S. Muskie. The Democratic party in Maine remains organizationally weak at the local level. In the state legislature Democrats divide into liberal and conservative camps on certain key issues (as do the Republicans). As a result, neither party in Maine yet offers a clearly defined position on state issues. At present, more state party systems seem to fit into the personality-oriented category than any other.

A very different type of state two-party system is one that John Fenton has styled the *job-oriented* two-party system. In a job-oriented state, "people who participate in politics on a day-to-day basis do so out of desire for jobs or contracts rather than because of a concern for public policy."[21] Fenton believes that Ohio, Indiana, and Illinois manifest this pattern. What causes a party to become job-oriented? For one thing, these states reflect a pronounced individualistic political culture wherein politics is regarded as a profession. An additional important factor is the presence in the same party of persons who disagree sharply on contemporary issues. The Democratic parties in the three states mentioned, for instance, are loose coalitions of, on the one hand, people with southern backgrounds who are generally conservative on public policy issues and, on the other, urban dwellers and ethnic minorities who take a more liberal stance on the same questions. Because of such divisions Democratic leaders in Ohio, Indiana, and Illinois have generally tried to avoid basing their campaigns on issues. Instead, they resort to promises of jobs and favors to keep their ranks together. Voting along party lines in the state legislature is usually higher in job-oriented states than in personality-oriented states, but much of the division between the parties revolves around questions affecting the prestige and power of the parties as organizations. Politicians generally do not win in these states because of their positions on public issues.

A final type of two-party alignment, the *issue-oriented* pattern, comes the closest of the six kinds of party systems to offering the voters some choice in public policy. Fenton classifies Michigan, Wisconsin, and Minnesota, three moralistic states, as issue-oriented two-party domains.[22] The principal differences among the political patterns in these states and those in Ohio, Indiana, and Illinois, apart from a greater general voter concern with public issues, is that the parties in these northern states are composed of people who are like-minded in their outlook on contemporary problems.

The presence of issue-oriented parties in Michigan, Wisconsin, and Minnesota is mainly — though not entirely — a postwar phenomenon. (Wisconsin's dominant Republican party revealed a continuing division over issues before World War II.) For many years all three states were strongly one-party Republican, with the Democratic party unable to wage effective state campaigns. Following the Second World War, groups of liberal and professional people took over the leadership of the moribund Democratic parties — best exemplified, perhaps, by the role of the United Auto Workers in the Michigan Democratic party. The result was to make both parties more attentive to issues. Also, the parties competed at all levels of government. No areas or offices in the states were permanently conceded by one party to the other — a phenomenon sometimes common in job-oriented states. Fenton thinks that the issue-oriented campaigns in Michigan, Wisconsin, and Minnesota have helped make them relatively generous in their public services. He notes that the level of public welfare expenditure, for instance, is considerably higher in these states (as measured by the portion of per capita income taxed and spent for welfare purposes) than it is in Illinois, Indiana, and Ohio.[23]

This discussion of types of state party systems can hardly do justice to the rich variety of party alignments in the states. It should, however, make clear that a simple classification of state parties into one- and two-party systems is only a first step in analysis and not in itself an especially accurate statement of a state's political life.

The Problem of Party Responsibility

Party alignments, as noted above, have been unusually dynamic in the states in the past decade. It may be appropriate, therefore, to conclude the discussion of state parties by raising the question of party responsibility. The idea of "responsible parties" has been discussed at length in both scholarly and popular literature. Definitions of the concept vary, but most scholars agree that a "responsible" party system is one in which the parties offer voters meaningful alternatives of public policy and, as reasonably cohesive political units, enact policy programs into law once elected to office. In the discussion of the types of state party systems, we noted that only the issue-oriented two-party arrangement appeared to approach the idea of "responsible party." We may thus ask: In light of the slowly increasing number of two-party states, will we witness an increase in the number of issue-oriented or "responsible" parties in the states? Or may we expect most state parties to remain mainly cadres of politicians who more often than not find ways to win office without taking stands on issues?

There can be little doubt that the revolution in political campaign techniques over the past two decades is producing significant changes in some of the party types. The extensive use of television and public relations, in particular, has made it difficult for most politicians to avoid at least some discussion of issues in campaigns. Politicians who could once rely on a hillbilly band to get them through a primary in a multifactional state, or on legions of faithful precinct workers to secure primary victory in a job-oriented two-party state, now find these resources less useful. During the 1970 Democratic primaries in the traditional job-oriented states of Ohio and Pennsylvania, for example, two candidates endorsed by the organization were defeated in statewide contests by insurgent candidates who relied mainly on television to convey their messages.[24] One result of the use of mass media in campaigns has been to simplify many pressing issues into slogans, best typified perhaps by the thirty-second television political commercial. Spending limits imposed on candidates for public office by some states in the aftermath of the Watergate scandals may reduce the usage of television in campaigns. Yet the broader impact of the mass media should not be lost sight of: some treatment of issues is now expected of candidates. Commenting on the changing campaign styles as they have emerged in one state (Texas), a political scientist writes:

> Along with the change in style has come a somewhat sharper focus. Candidates are more and more oriented to the issues. . . . There is still more than enough political verbiage, but the trend seems to be to demand a clearer position and less obscurantism from candidates. The result is perhaps a cleaner line of divisions at the polls, reflecting a sharper cleavage among Texas voters than was afforded in the past.[25]

Barriers to Responsible Parties. Certainly a major stumbling block to effective party governance in the states at the present time is the system of separation of powers. V. O. Key, Jr. aptly dubbed the separation of powers arrangement a "wondrous damper on party government."[26] The division of power between the executive and legislative branches often prevents state parties from achieving their full performance. In a pioneering study of thirty-two nonsouthern states for the years 1930 through 1952, Key found that "after one out of three elections . . . the governor was faced by a legislature with one or both houses controlled by the opposite party."[27] The incidence of divided party control in the states has increased in recent years as more and more states have become two-party. Following the 1970 elections twenty states (out of forty-eight having partisan legislatures) faced the dilemma of having the governorship in the hands of one party and at least one house of the legislature under the control of the other party. The comparable figure for the 1972 elections was twenty-three states. For 1974 it was nineteen states. We thus seem to be in a period in which one-third to one-half of the states at any given time are unable to attain the goal of party government along the lines of the classic "responsible party" model because of the operation of separation of powers.

Another problem in establishing responsible party government is related to the rise in the number of independent voters. The political turbulence of the 1960s led to serious voter alienation from both major parties. From 1964 to 1972 the portion of voters classifying themselves as independents increased sharply from 23 percent to 34 percent. Independents now constitute the second largest voting group in the country, considerably exceeding the number of Republican party affiliates. The increase in voter independence has not resulted in the election of many state officials labeling themselves as independent (about three-tenths of one percent of all state legislators are currently independents), but one state (Maine) in 1974 elected an independent as governor. The long-run impact of the decomposition of the parties will probably be a more fluid coalitional politics in state legislatures as public policy questions are resolved.

Perhaps the best summary of these political tendencies is to say that parties in the states will continue to be a major, but certainly not the only, link between the voters and the decision-making organs of state political systems. State political parties have never really dominated the input process in state politics. A broadly based and intense concern with the operation of state government — certainly necessary for disciplined "responsible" parties — has historically been absent in nearly all fifty states. As voter interest in the issues of state politics increases, so, we may argue, will the tendency of state parties to become more attentive to questions of public policy. In a broader sense, however, we may be moving toward a time when political parties in all democratic societies must content themselves with, as Frank Sorauf suggests, a role of "first among equals."[28] Sorauf argues that as the interests and loyalties of a democratic electorate become more diverse and heterogenous — a process clearly at work in most states — political parties alone will prove inadequate to organize them. Rather, the parties must compete with other organizing devices for the political loyalty and support of citizens. A major and long-standing competitor of political parties for such loyalty has been interest groups.

Interest Groups and State Politics

Broadside indictments of the conduct of state politics — a persistent theme in U. S. political commentary — have frequently been directed at the activities of state interest groups. An examination of the political processes in twelve of our larger states, prepared by a group of journalists in 1949, began with the assertion that "everywhere, state government is in the grip of minority or vested interests . . . , everywhere, there is gross lobby manipulation."[29] Whatever the degree of literary overkill involved here, this statement reflects the persistent impression that interest group exploitation and state politics are of a piece. In a survey of Washington lobbyists in the early 1960s, it was found that these lobbyists routinely assumed that lobbying in the states was a good deal more unsavory than comparable activity in Washington. State lobbying was, they felt, "cruder, more basic, more obvious, more freewheeling, on a lower plane and more open to corruption" than was the national process that they were involved in.[30]

Are these impressions correct? We do not have the empirical data to say for sure. There are few studies of interest group activity in the states, and even most of these do not make interstate or state-national comparisons in any systematic way. On the other hand, much of what has been noted so far in this text supports the idea that interest groups have consistently played a large role in state politics. That relatively few people have maintained an interest in state affairs and that "narrow governing coalitions" have emerged as a result are conditions that clearly contribute to interest group involvement in the political processes of the states. Two general characteristics of state political systems seem to permit private groups to be more influential at the state level than at the national. These characteristics involve matters of social composition and governmental structure. While we cannot prove or disprove the incidence of cruder or more corrupt direct lobbying in the states, we can make a case that interest groups as a whole probably have a greater effect on the policies of states than they do on those of the national government.

Comparisons of Social Composition. It is a truism that no U. S. state is as pluralistic and diversified as is the Union that it helps to form. In varying degrees all states manifest a greater homogeneity in their individual populations than does the nation as a whole. Studies have shown that interest groups tend to be strongest in areas that are socially homogeneous and in which a relatively small number of private groups is making demands on government.[31] In a sparsely populated rural area, for example, a single large company or corporation may wield inordinate amounts of political power within that area. On the other hand, interest groups appear to have somewhat less impact on public affairs in political systems containing many groups and organizations. As the number of competing groups increases, so do the opportunities for government officials to play the demands of one group off the claims of another. In such a situation no single group is likely to predominate.

The states, or at least a good many of them, traditionally have fit the first model; the United States as a whole probably best fits the second. Although there are vast differences in the power of American interest groups, scholars generally agree that there is no unified "ruling elite" in national politics. The great number of competing groups in national affairs helps to limit the power of any one. David Truman has observed that where many interest groups compete for people's interest and loyalty, overlapping memberships among these groups will tend to restrain their demands on one another and on government. He notes: "Given the problems of cohesion and internal group politics that result from overlapping membership, the emergence of a multiplicity of interest groups in itself contains no danger for the political system."[32]

Many of the smaller states seem to be sufficiently homogeneous in their social structures to correspond rather closely to the first model. One or two key economic groups may predominate simply because they have no real competition. An account of Wyoming politics, for example, points out that during the early and middle 1960s about one-half of Wyoming's state legislators held memberships in the Wyoming Stock Growers Association.[33] This is a very high percentage of state legislators to be members of one interest group. The Stock Growers Association has been rather small (in 1965 it had a total membership of 2,600 people or about 1 percent of Wyoming's population). But certain factors have clearly worked to its advantage. For one thing, Wyoming's total economy is heavily dependent on cattle production. For another, the state's population is very small. Also, the population is transient (in the 1960 census Wyoming was the only state to have more than 50 percent of its native-born citizens residing in other states). Partly as a result of these factors the Stock Growers Association has managed over the years to develop a large "built-in" lobby with the Wyoming legislature.

Delaware is another state that has a single interest group taking an unusually active hand in state affairs. The group is composed of the executives and employees of the E. I. Du Pont Company, who make up about 11 percent of the state's work force. In 1970 legislators with connections to Du Pont chaired nearly one-third of the standing committees of the state house and senate and had about half the seats on the Delaware legislature's most powerful body, the Joint Finance Committee. A Ralph Nader study group exploring Delaware politics concluded that Du Pont's power is due to "the corporate establishment's near monopoly over the important political resources: people, time, expertise, money, and media."[34] A Du Pont employee who held public office normally received 20 percent of his or her working time off with pay.

Most states, even the smaller ones, are more diversified in their economic and social life than Wyoming and Delaware. For that reason the examples of the Stock Growers Association and the Du Pont Company may be a bit unusual. But the notion of social composition can also be applied to different levels in the state political system, such as the individual state legislative district. Because state legislative districts are typically a great deal smaller and more socially homogeneous than congressional districts, the opportunities for a single interest group to influence a legislator through constituency pressure would appear greater at the state level than at the national. This idea could hold true even if — unlike the example of Wyoming — there were some semblance of competition among groups on a statewide basis.

Although data on state-national comparisons are meager, the

available evidence certainly suggests the general accuracy of this point. A revealing study was done by John Kingdon, who conducted a survey of candidates for state and federal offices in Wisconsin in 1964.[35] Kingdon found that nearly three times more state legislative candidates than congressional candidates labeled an interest group as the "most" important group for their electoral success in that year. Wisconsin candidates for the U. S. Congress tended to rely more heavily on volunteer organizations and to use the mass media more extensively in their campaigns. The small, usually homogeneous districts of Wisconsin state legislators and the low visibility of their office contributed to the importance of interest groups in their electoral coalitions. Kingdon speculates that these differences in the influence of interest groups in political campaigns have a bearing on public policy:

> One reasonable inference one may draw from these findings is that a state legislator, more than a congressman . . . takes account of the crucial members of his supporting coalition in the making of public policy. Because he believes that they are so important to him in terms of his re-election chances, he cannot afford to slight them as much as could a representative who does not place as great an importance on them.[36]

Comparisons of Governmental Structure. A second factor permitting more intensive involvement of interest groups in state affairs than in national politics is the structure of state government. Many states do not resemble the federal bureaucratic model, in which the president as chief executive names (with Senate concurrence) the members of his cabinet. In the states, governors can appoint some department heads, but the chiefs of many key departments, bureaus, and commissions win office in ways distinctly independent of gubernatorial control. One mode of appointment, favored in some rural states, is selection of a bureau or department head by a committee composed, entirely or in part, of persons the agency directly serves. This guarantees certain interest groups in the state at least a veto on the people who are to regulate their affairs. Consider, for instance, the case of the state health officer in Alabama.[37] This official is appointed by the Alabama State Board of Health. But the board of health is nothing more than, ex officio, the Medical Association of Alabama. As a result, the Alabama State Health Officer is effectively responsible to a single interest group, the Medical Association of Alabama. Grant McConnell summarizes the general pattern in state bureaucracies in this way: "The machinery of state administration has made an extensive accommodation to the demands of particular groups, [and] this accommodation has amounted to a parceling out of public authority to private groups."[38]

State legislatures reveal certain structural features that make them more amenable to lobbying influence than is the U. S. Congress. State legislators are more likely than U. S. congressmen to be amateur politicians: they are paid much less for their work; they generally meet less often; and they have few of the staff services that U. S. congressmen enjoy. All these conditions serve to heighten the impact of lobbyists on state legislative processes. An analysis of lobbyist-legislator relationships in Oregon, Utah, Massachusetts, and North Carolina provides illustrative data. The surveys found that in these states "the mean experience of lobbyists exceeds by far that of legislators."[39] In North Carolina and Utah, for instance, typical lobbyists had been at their jobs twice as long as had typical legislators. Moreover, in the four states studied, lobbyists on the average had attained a higher educational level than had legislators. Perhaps most important, both legislators and lobbyists in these states agreed, in interviews, that lobbyists were "more professional" in their work than legislators. The strength of lobbyists is based primarily on their superior knowledge of issues of public policy affecting specific groups. Because of a shortage of state legislative staffs, legislators may have few other sources of relevant information.

Interest Groups and Policy. The significance of lobbyists does vary with different types of issues. In a fifty-state survey, state legislators indicated that they relied heavily on lobbyists' advice about policies dealing with liquor, labor relations, business, agricultural issues, water resources, gambling, and social welfare.[40] Legislators consulted interest groups less frequently about state finances, legislative apportionment, health programs, general state administration, civil rights, and highway policies. As an example of this, the rapid rise of state public expenditures since World War II has sometimes occurred in the face of strenuous opposition by conservative, probusiness interests and their spokesmen in state capitals.

In general, however, organized interest groups seem to play a larger role in aggregating the needs of citizens in the states than they do in the national arena. In recent years two controversial areas in which laws have differed among the states are aid to parochial schools and right-to-work laws. Interest groups appear to have had an impact on producing these policy variations.[41] As of 1965 the twenty-one states providing or permitting some form of textbook or transportation assistance for parochial schools had a considerably higher proportion of Roman Catholics than did the twenty-nine states which did not provide such assistance. In the area of labor relations, the seventeen states which in 1965 prohibited the use of union/shop contracts between labor and management that require a worker to join a union as a condition of employment had a lower AFL-CIO membership (as a percentage of the civilian labor force) than the thirty-three states that had no such provision. The AFL-CIO is strongly opposed to right-to-work laws and has been able to prevent their passage in the large industrial states in which its membership is substantial.

Of course, the impact exerted by interest groups as a whole varies widely from state to state. Among the factors that determine the effectiveness of private groups in a state political system, political parties are perhaps the most important. Political scientists for some time have recognized that the strength of interest groups in a state is likely to vary inversely with the strength of its party system. In the mid-1950s, Belle Zeller asked observers in each of the then forty-eight states to rate the interest-group system in that state as "strong," "moderate," or "weak." Her findings from this survey generally support the idea that interest groups hold greatest sway in one-party systems and are somewhat less weighty in two-party states. Of the twenty-four states Zeller found to have "strong" interest groups, seventeen fell into the category of one-party or one-party modified states according to a classification of state party systems focusing on the period of the 1950s.[42] Included in the group of seventeen states were all the states of the Old Confederacy except Virginia and, additionally, Oklahoma, Kentucky, Arizona, New Mexico, Wisconsin, Iowa, and Maine. On the other hand, the twenty-one dominions Zeller discovered to contain "moderate" or "weak" pressure systems generally were states with competitive parties. States in this group, including New York, New Jersey, Pennsylvania, Ohio, Indiana, and Illinois, were characterized by the presence of large numbers of competing interests as well as durable two-party systems. As two-partyism gradually spreads to more states, the ability of private groups to dominate the mobilization of power in individual states will likely diminish. Interest groups are more inclined to channel their demands through the parties when there is a viable, competitive two-party arrangement.

At the same time significant changes are taking place in the interest groups themselves in the states. Traditional economic groups will continue to be important, and may become even more active. An article that appeared in the *Harvard Business Review* in 1974 called attention to the rising importance of the states in the federal system, warning that "business has too often ignored the altered composition of state government and the powerful new forces working at that level."[43] But quite different groups are forming and moving into positions of influence around state governments. One type of association is composed of municipal and county officials. These public officials have entered state politics in much the same manner that state governors (as we noted in chapter 2) have sought access at the national level. In Connecticut, local representatives from the state's thirty largest cities have established a lobby at the state capital.[44] New Jersey's seven largest cities and their mayors have organized to work at the state level. More than one-tenth of all lobbyists registered before the California legislature in 1972 represented governmental units, either individually or collectively. These groups are concerned with such questions as state tax policies and the rights and powers of municipal bureaucracies and municipal unions. Their activity is an outgrowth of the expanding public sector as represented by urban government.

A different kind of interest group that is relatively new in state politics is the consumer or "public interest" lobby. Since 1970 the citizens' organization known as Common Cause has developed affiliates in the states and has pursued state government reform as part of its national program. The organization takes some credit for the adoption in more than half the states of statutes requiring detailed financial disclosures by certain public officials.[45] The organization also has encouraged strict enforcement of lobbyist disclosure provisions that now exist in most states. These and other "public interest" associations tend to challenge the power of some traditional economic groups. In 1970 the state of Maine, which in the Zeller survey was listed as having strong interest groups (mostly pulp and paper and private power companies), enacted a far-reaching series of antipollution measures and set up a Coastal Protection Fund paid for by industry. Broadly based conservation organizations in Maine provided the impetus for these moves, which are currently taking place in many other states.

The widening of pressure group activity to include interests of other than established economic groups may be the most significant development in the 1970s in the states concerning the input agencies of state politics. Even though reapportionment has led the states to become more responsive to their citizens, the influence of public opinion on decision makers is limited by the complexities and shifting nature of specific issues. Two-partyism, and the choice of candidates that it implies, is taking hold in an increasing number of states, but widespread voter alienation from the parties — a fairly recent phenomenon — casts doubt on how well the parties as organizations can compel private groups to work through them. It is in the emerging pluralism of interest groups, both material and idealistic, that issues may be most effectively focused on state decision makers.

State Constitutions

A useful way to analyze the impact of parties and interest groups — in broad outline — on a state's politics is to examine the state's constitution. Inspection of the constitutions of most states reveals not only the formal governmental structure of the particular dominion, but also something of its politics and informal power structure. All U. S. constitutions — federal, state, and local — resemble one another in certain superficial ways. As does the federal Constitution, for example, the typical state constitution establishes the general outlines of government, spells out the functions and duties of the several branches, and specifies the procedures for filling public offices. Yet the student of state politics should be aware of significant differences between the U. S. Constitution and state constitutions. A discussion of two points of variation may delineate the distinct type of politics surrounding the operation of state constitutions.

State and National Charters Compared. One vital, but sometimes overlooked, distinction between the federal Constitution and state constitutions is that state charters are more "majoritarian" than the federal model. Voters and politicians in the states have generally played a large and direct role in shaping the language of the constitutional document. More than half of the states (thirty-one) have discarded their original constitutions (under which they entered the Union) and have written new ones. Louisiana has had eleven constitutions; Georgia is currently governed by its eighth constitution; Alabama, Florida, and Virginia have had six each. In these states it is almost true that each generation has written its own constitution. Moreover, in nearly all the states, popular majorities have amended their constitutions much more frequently than the nation as a whole has modified the U. S. Constitution. As of 1976 constitutions in the fifty states carried a median number of sixty-three constitutional amendments each, a figure that is more than double the number (twenty-six) of national amendments. And these twenty-six amendments took 187 years to become established, while state constitutions are usually much younger. In the typical state it is an unusual election day — and an even more exceptional regular session of the state legislature — when proposals for altering the state constitution are not up for judgment.

Majorities have at times, of course, significantly modified the U. S. Constitution. The income tax provision added by the Sixteenth Amendment and the due process and equal protection clauses of the Fourteenth Amendment equip the national government with some of its most critical powers. But the larger point in comparing state constitutions with the national model is that much of the work of keeping the U. S. Constitution up to date falls to the U. S. Supreme Court. That is, it is the responsibility of a judicial elite. When the national government in the 1930s moved from a laissez-faire to a welfare conception of its responsibilities in regulating the national economy, it did so without making a single change in the Constitution. The politics surrounding that change, so far as the Constitution was concerned, involved mainly a shift in doctrine on the part of the Supreme Court. One probable reason that state electorates have not been willing to permit state judges as extensive a role as Supreme Court justices in interpreting constitutions is that the states have never accorded their own constitutions the sanctity generally given the national instrument. State political groups have tended to regard state constitutions as only a bit, if any, higher than regular statute law.

A second difference between state and federal constitutions involves their main purposes. Historically, the federal government and local government grew out of delegations of power from the states. The national government would have no legal authority whatsoever if the Constitution did not exist. Through that instrument in 1789 the states delegated some of their powers to the national government, and the stipulations of this agreement constitute the legal basis for the exercise of national power. The states, on the other hand, historically derived their power from a different source. State governments assumed all the powers exercised over them by the British government at the time they declared themselves independent colonies in 1776. Thus the powers of state governments are limited only by the delegations that the states have made to another government (such as the federal government) and by prohibitions written into state constitutions forbidding certain actions. As one specialist puts it, state constitutions "do not *confer* powers on the state governments; they only *limit* the discretion of state officials."[46] Apart from those provisions dealing with the organization of state government, the text of the typical state constitution is weighted heavily with language telling state officials, especially members of the legislature, what they cannot do.

These "majoritarian" and "limiting" features of state constitutions provide a useful way of looking at the politics of constitutionalism in the states. Essentially, we may regard the politics of state constitutions as a process wherein voters, parties, and interest groups struggle over the question of how greatly the powers and discretion of state government should be limited. Various state political organizations have long sought to write into the state charters provisions prohibiting the legislature from interfering with their economic interests. In about half of the states, for instance, highway interest groups have succeeded in securing adoption of constitutional clauses prohibiting or restricting the use of highway revenues (for example, from gasoline taxes) for purposes not associated with road building and maintenance.[47]

In a number of states the constitutional victories won by political groups are reflected in detailed constitutional language. California, for instance, is not permitted to tax ownership of certain types of "fruit and nut-bearing trees under the age of four years." Oklahoma's constitution provides that the flash test for all kerosene oil for illuminating purposes "shall be 115 degrees Fahrenheit." In New York the constitution mandates that the state's forest preserve must be "forever kept as wild forest land."[48] An analysis of state charters found that those states having "strong" interest groups (according to the Zeller survey) generally had the lengthiest (and most detailed) constitutions.[49] Georgia's document leads in size with about one-half million words (about ten times the length of this book); until 1974 Louisiana's constitution had about 255,000 words; and Alabama, Oklahoma, and Texas presently each have fundamental charters exceeding 50,000 words. The typical state constitution is about three times longer than the U. S. Constitution. The political consequences of the excessive, and often contradictory, detail written into the basic document are very much the same in all states: state officials are deprived of a flexibility in dealing with current problems that most observers regard as a prerequisite to vigorous and responsible state government.

Constitutional Revision in the States. In most states the content of the constitutional document is a lively contentious issue. During the seven-year period from 1966 to 1972, according to one authority, "at least two-thirds of the states took steps directly toward general constitutional revision, in addition to the usual piecemeal amendments."[50] The main impetus behind the current willingness of the states to consider modification of their constitutions seems to be related to the reapportionment decisions of the U. S. Supreme Court. Rural groups in the states had long opposed the idea of holding constitutional conventions out of fear that new legislative apportionment provisions would be a major consequence. When this issue was defused by the Supreme Court in its "one man, one vote" rulings, their hostility to revision partially subsided.

What have been the results of the current wave of constitution writing in the states? Probably the greatest changes have taken place in those constitutional articles spelling out the organization and powers of the state legislative, executive, and judicial systems. States have removed or raised their debt limits and have paved the way for legislative enactment of new forms of taxation. The authority of the governor in some states has been strengthened, and the term of office extended. Efforts have been made to streamline the state judiciary. The general direction of reform has been to reduce the number of detailed limitations imposed on state governments by earlier generations of voters and their legislatures. The new provisions are usually shorter and more general than the portions replaced.

In a number of states, constitutional change has been a politically explosive subject. Segments of the state electorates who have vested interests in existing constitutions have resisted fundamental modification. Rural groups in particular have seemed to be hostile to attempts to write a wholly new constitution through a state constitutional convention called for that purpose. In a 1968 referendum held to approve a new state constitution (which opponents denounced as elitist, intellectual, and biased toward blacks), rural voters in Maryland, who constituted 21 percent of the electorate, cast 29 percent of the opposition votes.[51] Partly because of rural opposition, the record of state adoptions of new constitutions over the past decade has been uneven: citizens have approved new documents in Connecticut (1965), Florida (1968), Illinois (1970), North Carolina (1970), Virginia (1970), Montana (1972), and Louisiana (1974), but have turned down constitutions in New York (1967), Rhode Island (1968), Maryland (1968), New Mexico (1969), Arkansas (1970), and North Dakota (1972). On the other hand, voters have been more willing to approve individual constitutional amendments, which are usually proposed to the electorate by the state legislature. Of some 1,825 constitutional changes proposed in the states between 1966 and 1972, citizens approved 1,293, or 71 percent.[52] Nearly all segments of the states' electorates have agreed on the need for constitutional modifications in such areas as financial administration, conservation and the environment, and local government powers. Approval rates of amendments associated with these topics exceeded 80 percent in the states from 1966 to 1972.

The politics of constitutional change in the states reveals the continuing influence — at least in a general way — of the states' most attentive constituents: rural, small-town, and middle-class voters have accepted limited modifications through piecemeal amendments, but they have been suspicious of efforts to radically transform state government under new constitutions. At the same time, the fact that pressures for change have been intense may be attributed to a heightened interest by urban groups in state politics. City and suburban residents often have led efforts to streamline state constitutions. Their communities are usually most in need of new state action and assistance; their work in improving state charters is a step toward more effective state policy making.

Summary

This chapter has examined the principal input agencies of state politics, and has concluded with an analysis of their impact on state constitutions. The agencies transmitting the demands and requests of citizens in the states are reflective of state political environments. As these environments have changed over time, so, too, have the vehicles communicating public concerns shown alteration. Two particularly important environmental factors in shaping state input agencies are the limited visibility of state politics and the states' social compositions.

The limited attention traditionally paid to state affairs by state electorates has long weakened the effectiveness of one input agency — public opinion — as a device for transmitting ideas into public policy. The overall congruence between state public opinion on various issues and the actual policies of the individual states has not been high. However, in those instances where issues are closely linked to particular state environments, a substantial level of congruence or fit has seemed to exist.

The significance of the factor of social composition may be seen in the development of political parties and interest groups. Historically the greater social homogeneity of the states (compared to the nation) led them to have a preponderance of one-party systems and to rely on economic interest groups as the principal channels through which citizen needs were aggregated and focused on state decision makers. In more recent years, developments such as interstate migration and increased citizen sensitivity to issues have contributed to a spread of two-partyism in the states. At the same time, interest group activity has broadened to include governmental and public associations, which organizations may be of increasing importance in future years in shaping state programs.

Changes in input agencies in the states have speeded the process of state constitutional revision. When economic interest groups were most powerful, state charters were usually lengthy documents studded with the policy preferences of these groups. In the past decade, the emergence of a more broadly based state politics has led to the modernization of state constitutions, especially to the relaxation of restrictions on state decision makers. It is to these officials, and their work in setting programs and policies for the states, that we turn next.

NOTES

1. A. H. Birch, *Representative and Responsible Government* (Toronto: University of Toronto Press, 1964), p. 171.
2. Robert E. Lane and David O. Sears, *Public Opinion* (Englewood Cliffs, N.J.: Prentice-Hall, 1964), p. 61.
3. See Ronald E. Weber, Anne H. Hopkins, Michael L. Mezey, and Frank J. Munger,

"Computer Simulation of State Electorates," *Public Opinion Quarterly*, 36, No. 4 (Winter 1972–1973), 549–565.

4. Frank J. Munger, "Opinions, Elections, Parties, and Policies: A Cross-State Analysis." Paper delivered at the Annual Meeting of the American Political Science Association, New York, New York, September 2–6, 1969.

5. Richard L. Sutton, "The States and the People: Measuring and Accounting for 'State Representativeness,' " *Polity*, 5, No. 4 (Summer 1973), 465–466.

6. Poll data are drawn from Munger, "Opinions, Elections, Parties, and Policies," pp. 7–12.

7. Ibid.

8. Sutton, "The States and the People," p. 465.

9. V. O. Key, Jr., *Public Opinion and American Democracy* (New York: Alfred A. Knopf, 1961), p. 536.

10. E. E. Schattschneider, *Party Government* (New York: Holt, Rinehart, and Winston, 1942), p. 1.

11. Cornelius P. Cotter and Bernard C. Hennessy, *Politics Without Power: The National Party Committees* (New York: Atherton Press, 1964), p. 40.

12. *The Book of the States*, 1974–1975 (Lexington, Ky.: The Council of State Governments, 1974).

13. Austin Ranney, "Parties in State Politics," in Herbert Jacob and Kenneth N. Vines, eds., *Politics in the American States*, 2nd ed. (Boston: Little, Brown, 1971), pp. 82–121.

14. Figures are drawn from *The Book of the States* from 1946 through 1975. Minnesota and Nebraska, which had nonpartisan elections for most of this period (Minnesota legislators ran on a party ticket for the first time in 1972), and Alaska and Hawaii (which were not in the Union for the full period) are omitted from the analysis.

15. Ranney, "Parties in State Politics," p. 92.

16. V. O. Key, Jr., *Southern Politics in State and Nation* (New York: Knopf, 1949), p. 36.

17. Ibid, p. 19.

18. Allan P. Sindler, "Bifactional Rivalry as an Alternative to Two-Party Competition in Louisiana," *American Political Science Review*, 49 (September 1955), 641–662.

19. Malcolm E. Jewell and Everett W. Cunningham, *Kentucky Politics* (Lexington, Ky.: University of Kentucky Press, 1968), p. 132.

20. William Buchanan, *Legislative Partisanship: The Deviant Case of California* (Berkeley: University of California Press, 1963).

21. John H. Fenton, *Midwest Politics* (New York: Holt, Rinehart, and Winston, 1966), pp. 115ff.

22. Ibid., pp. 9ff.

23. Ibid., p. 230.

24. The successful candidates were Milton Shapp (Pa.) and Howard Metzenbaum (Ohio). In the general election, Shapp won the governorship but Robert Taft, Jr. defeated Metzenbaum for the U. S. Senate.

25. Clifton McCleskey, *The Government and Politics of Texas*, 3rd ed. (Boston: Little, Brown, 1969), pp. 117–118.

26. V. O. Key, Jr., *American State Politics: An Introduction* (New York: Knopf, 1956), p. 52.

27. Ibid., pp. 53ff.

28. Frank J. Sorauf, *Party Politics in America* (Boston: Little, Brown, 1968), p. 430.

29. Robert S. Allen, ed., *Our Sovereign States* (New York: Vanguard Press, 1949), p. xii.

30. Lester Milbrath, *The Washington Lobbyists* (Chicago: Rand McNally, 1963), pp. 302–303.

31. Harmon Zeigler, "Interest Groups in the States," in Jacob and Vines, eds., *Politics in the American States*, 2nd ed. (Boston: Little, Brown, 1971), pp. 113–128.

32. David B. Truman, *The Governmental Process* (New York: Knopf, 1951), p. 510.

33. T. A. Larson, *History of Wyoming* (Lincoln: University of Nebraska Press, 1965), p. 578.

34. James Phelan and Robert Poxen, *The Company State* (New York: Grossman Publishers, 1973), p. 304.
35. John W. Kingdon, *Candidates for Office: Beliefs and Strategies* (New York: Random House, 1966).
36. Ibid., p. 139.
37. Grant McConnell, *Private Power and American Democracy* (New York: Knopf, 1967), p. 188.
38. Ibid., p. 189.
39. Harmon Zeigler and Michael Baer, *Lobbying: Interaction and Influence in American State Legislatures* (Belmont, Calif.: Wadsworth, 1969), p. 61.
40. Wayne R. Francis, "A Profile of Legislator Perception of Interest Group Behavior Relating to Legislative Issues in the States," *Western Political Quarterly*, 24, No. 4 (December 1971), 702–712.
41. The opinion data in this paragraph are drawn from Munger, "Opinions, Elections, Parties, and Policies." For a conceptual treatment of the relative importance of state input agencies, including public opinion and interest groups, on state public policies, see Ronald E. Weber and William R. Shaffer, "Public Opinion and American State Policy-Making," *Midwest Journal of Political Science*, 16, No. 4 (November 1972), 683–699.
42. Belle Zeller, *American State Legislatures* (New York: Thomas Y. Crowell, 1954), pp. 190–191. Idaho, New Hampshire, and North Dakota were not classified.
43. Martin R. Haley and James M. Kiss, "Larger Stakes in Statehouse Lobbying," *Harvard Business Review*, 52 (January 1974), 126.
44. Donald H. Haider, *When Governments Come to Washington* (New York: Free Press, 1974), p. 301.
45. Thomas S. Belford and Bruce Adams, "Conflict of Interest Legislation and the Common Cause Model Act," *Municipal Year Book* (Washington, D.C.: International City Management Association, 1975), pp. 170–176.
46. Herbert Kaufman, *Politics and Policies in State and Local Governments* (Englewood Cliffs, N.J.: Prentice-Hall, 1963), p. 37.
47. Robert S. Friedman, "State Politics and Highways," in Herbert Jacob and Kenneth N. Vines, eds., *Politics in the American States*, 2nd ed. (Boston: Little, Brown, 1971), p. 495.
48. These and other examples are in David R. Morgan and Samuel A. Kirkpatrick, eds., *Constitutional Revision: Cases and Commentary* (Norman, Okla.: University of Oklahoma—Bureau of Governmental Research, 1970).
49. Lewis A. Froman, Jr., "Some Effects of Interest Groups in State Politics," *American Political Science Review*, 60 (December, 1966), 952–962.
50. Albert L. Sturm, *Trends in State Constitution-Making, 1966–72* (Lexington, Ky.: The Council of State Governments, 1973), pp. 1–2.
51. John P. Wheeler, Jr. et al., *Magnificent Failure: The Maryland Constitutional Convention of 1967-1968* (New York: National Municipal League, 1970), p. 212.
52. Sturm, *Trends*, p. 43.

Chapter IV

THE AUTHORITATIVE DECISION-MAKING AGENCIES

In the four-part systems model used to organize this discussion of state politics, the agencies that set down the authoritative values or policies for the states constitute the third segment. In the United States these agencies are readily identifiable as legislatures, executives, and courts. Generally, their function is to convert the demands that rise from the states' environments into laws and programs that attempt to satisfy these demands. This chapter scrutinizes the relationship of the decision-making agencies to the dimensions of state politics already discussed. How do these agencies respond to the states' environments and how effective are they in meeting the demands placed on them? Because reform of state government has been a topic of heated debate in recent times, this chapter will try to provide a context in which the goals of specific reform measures can be understood. The discussion here should form a basis for the treatment of the substantive policies of the states in the concluding chapter.

State Legislatures

State legislatures occupy an ambiguous place in the political systems of states. On the one hand, they are honored as being the "people's" branch of state government, a label carrying majestic importance in a democratic society. The legislature is normally described first in the state constitution. State legislatures can trace their histories back to the colonial assemblies that emerged in 1776 as the first independent organs of governments in the United States. Legislatures traditionally have been regarded as the place where the great political issues of states must finally be resolved. On the other hand, state legislatures in modern times have frequently been thought of as the "sick men" of the American governmental system. Critical commentary about them and political cartooning of them abound. "It would be easy," observes one writer, "to get the idea that bib overalls, raucous jokes, country ballads, ready fists, and an eccentric sense of priority in debating the public business characterize all state legislators all the time."[1]

It is instructive to contrast state legislatures with the U. S. Congress. We could spell out a large number of differences in the operations of state assemblies as compared with those of the Congress, but most of these may better be brought under a single broad concept of social science that has proved fruitful in investigating political institutions in general. We may argue that as a legislative body Congress seems to be much more *institutionalized* than are most state legislatures. Although it is a somewhat elusive concept, the idea of institutionalization refers mainly to the degree of professionalism, stability, or permanence that a political organization exhibits. In a revealing study, Nelson Polsby found greater institutionalization to be one of the most notable changes in the U. S. House of Representatives over the past century and a half.[2] Polsby's analysis is valuable to the student of state legislatures as well as to congressional scholars, for certain of the indicators he uses to measure the growth of institutionalization in the House are also applicable to state assemblies.

On what kinds of data does Polsby rely to show that the House of Representatives is more institutionalized today than it was a century ago? One source is the nature of congressional personnel. The author maintains that in a highly institutionalized body the membership is relatively stable, many members devote their careers to that body, and leaders are recruited from within the organization, usually after a long apprenticeship. By these criteria, Polsby shows that the House has changed drastically since the first part of the nineteenth century. In the early 1800s, the turnover rate of members approached 50 percent; the typical congressman served only a little longer than two terms; and the men elected to the Speakership characteristically spent no more than six years in the House prior to their elevation to the post.[3] In contrast to these patterns, the House of Representatives in the years since World War II has had a much more stable membership. During this period the turnover rate fell to about 20 percent; the average congressman served between five and six terms in office; and the three men elected to the Speakership between 1945 and 1965 each had more than twenty years of prior service in the House.[4] Thus, from 1789 to 1965 the House gradually but steadily developed a career membership; it became more institutionalized.

A second set of data that Polsby uses to test the degree of institutionalization concerns the internal arrangements of powers and duties in the House of Representatives. He argues that a highly institutionalized organization is relatively complex in its operations in the sense that there is a division of labor among its members and a formal separation of the functions that the organization performs. Although data are harder to come by in this area, Polsby thinks that key changes in the standing committee system in the House point to the growth of internal complexity. In the nineteenth century committee chairmen were appointed each session by party and factional leaders, and the committees were largely tools of whatever political groups were in command of the House.[5] Since the revolt against a dictatorial House Speaker (Joseph Cannon) in 1910 – 1911, committee chairmen have been selected mainly through the automatic workings of the seniority system. This change in the method of naming committee chairmen has vastly increased the powers of the committees. Protected by seniority, the standing committees in the House have been specialized "little legislatures"; they have acquired large staff facilities; and they have secured a nearly autonomous position in the House. The House committees in recent decades have been subject "only to very infrequent reversals and modifications of their powers by House party leaders."[6] The increasingly specialized role played by the standing committees is additional evidence of the growth of institutionalization in the House.

What is the connection between Polsby's analysis of the House of Representatives and U. S. state legislatures? Principally this: Many state legislatures today seem to be at about the same level of institutionalization as the U. S. House was in the early nineteenth century. Let us evaluate state legislatures according to Polsby's two indicators: the nature of legislative personnel and the level of internal legislative complexity.

Legislative Personnel. A chronic dilemma in most state legislatures is the high turnover of members. In the late 1930s a survey covering about one-fifth of the states found that the percentage of new members was approximately 40 percent for lower houses and 20 percent for state senates.[7] A study of all the states for the period from 1963 to 1971 determined that the turnover rates for upper and lower houses for those years had become similar: the average percentage of freshmen legislators in the fifty state senates in those years was 30.4; the portion of new members in state houses of representatives was 36.1 percent per legislative session.[8] Legislative redistricting in certain states in the 1960s seemed to compound already unstable membership situations. In Maine, for instance, a high turnover rate in the state senate for the period from 1963 to 1971 appeared partly due to a fundamental reapportionment in 1966 that changed the basis of state senatorial elections from counties to individual districts. It is true that the states generally have a greater membership stability in their legislatures than they did in the nineteenth century (historical research on the states of Wisconsin, Michigan, and Connecticut indicates that the portion of new legislators per session declined from over 70 percent in the 1890s to about 30 percent in the 1950s and 1960s).[9] Overall, however, the turnover rate in state legislatures remains nearly double that of the U. S. Congress.[10] One reason that state legislatures seem so frequently under fire may be that they typically lack a corps of career legislators able to reply effectively to criticism. Relatively few state legislators identify their own political welfare with that of the legislature as an institution.

There appear to be three general causes of the high turnover of legislators in the states. One involves personal finances. Until very recently, no state paid its legislators what could be called a living wage, and many still do not. For state legislators the job of serving their state and district often creates a severe financial burden. As one state assemblyman described the problem to an interviewer:

> Any way you look at it, the job means a sacrifice to you, your home, and your business. Most people don't realize that there are continual demands on your time outside the legislative sessions as well. I don't intend to make a career of politics.[11]

A second cause for the voluntary retirement of many legislators is psychological. Some men and women elected to state assemblies each session turn out to be poorly adapted to legislative life and wish to step down. At the end of the 1959 session of the Connecticut House of Representatives, James Barber queried ninety-six freshmen members about their reactions to their first term. He asked them specifically: "As of today, how likely is it that you would be willing to serve three or more terms in the Assembly in the future?"[12] One-third of the legislators replied that they either "probably" or "definitely" would not consider serving for that period. For a variety of reasons, this sizable group of assemblymen had become disenchanted with the legislative process in their first year in office.

Some of the people in this group were lawyer-legislators (Barber calls them "advertisers") whose main goal in getting elected had been to obtain free publicity for their law practice back home. Intensely concerned with their own careers, these legislators tended to be frustrated by the demands of deliberation and compromise in the work of the assembly. Other legislators who wanted to step down included elderly men and women, mostly from small towns, who had been persuaded to run for the legislature by local party leaders. These people (Barber calls them "reluctants") had family names and family reputations that party leaders thought would build attractive local tickets. Once in the legislature, the reluctants found the controversy and pressures of the job distasteful.

A third cause of high legislative turnover in the states is strictly political. Some of the most competent and dedicated legislators regard service in the state legislature as a steppingstone to higher public office. The typical state assembly has little of the appeal as a career institution that the U. S. Congress does. In a 1967 survey of 97 of the 110 members of the Michigan House of Representatives, one investigator found that a high proportion (82 percent) of these legislators stated a willingness to remain in the Michigan legislature for three or more terms.[13] But he discovered that more than half of the Michigan legislators (59 percent) *also* indicated an interest in seeking higher public office. These upwardly mobile legislators were among the best educated and most active in the Michigan lower house. Given the low status of the legislature in state politics, however, their service could be expected to be brief.

Legislative Complexity. One principal way, then, in which state legislatures differ from the U. S. Congress is that they are not able to attract and maintain a permanent corps of career members. This fluidity of membership in state legislatures has a variety of consequences in the conduct of state government. Perhaps the most immediate of these is seen in the internal operation of the state legislative bodies. The typical state legislature reveals none of the elaborate and systematic distribution of roles and powers among its members that — as was noted in the Polsby study — characterizes the U. S. House of Representatives. To use the language of our central concept, state assemblies in their internal operations are much less institutionalized than Congress.

Although it is a commonplace that the standing committees in Congress are where the "real work" is done, this is by no means true in all the states. For several reasons state legislative committees enjoy less autonomy and power to make decisions than their federal counterparts do. For one thing, the seniority principle is followed less closely in state legislatures than it is in Congress. Committee chairmen win their positions in the state legislatures in great part according to their favor with the presiding officers. A state legislator rarely has a prescriptive right to a committee chairmanship based solely on length of service on the committee. In addition, because of the relatively high turnover in the states, few legislators on a particular committee can claim more expertise in the area of the committee's work than that found in the legislative chamber as a whole. Finally, the states generally do not assign extensive staff facilities to their standing committees to permit these units to undertake investigations and to hold detailed hearings. Standing committees in most states are able to act as the major drafters of private and local bills, and they are often empowered to delay or to kill legislation. However, the committees generally cannot take credit for the preparation and passage of the major policy bills of a legislative session.

The fifty states do differ in the powers and responsibilities assigned to their committees, of course. Alan Rosenthal has examined state committee practices and has classified the performances of state legislative committees.[14] Better performing committees in his analysis were units that carefully screened bills reported to them (relatively few bills were reported to the floor), frequently amended bills before reporting them to the chambers, enjoyed a high rate of success in having their bills passed, and continued to function between legislative sessions. The states that seemed to have the most effective committees by these criteria were California, Iowa, Minnesota, North Dakota, Oklahoma, Florida, Nevada, Washington, West Virginia, and Wisconsin. Poorer performing committees existed in such states as Alabama, Delaware, Massachusetts, Missouri, Rhode Island, Georgia, Indiana, and New Jersey. Rosenthal believes that two factors, institutional capacity and institutional power, largely determine the performance of a state's committee system. Institutional capacity refers to the resources available to the standing committees. Better performing committee systems generally had professional staffs, and the committees themselves were limited in number so that legislators serving on them might specialize in their work. Institutional power relates primarily to the distribution of power in the legislature. States having strong committee systems usually revealed a greater decentralization or dispersion of power in the legislative body than states with less effective committees.

In those states with relatively weak committees, the critical work on legislation usually takes place after a bill has been reported from the committee. Political power in these state legislatures is often centralized in party caucuses (in two-party states) or in factional groupings (in one-party states). In many two-party states, caucuses of the two parties in each house review all major legislation between the time it is reported from committee and the occasion for debate and voting on the floor. In Pennsylvania in the 1960s, the standing committees rarely held hearings on bills submitted by the governor when his party controlled the legislature. Instead, these bills were reported to the floor — sometimes within a day or two of introduction — and were worked out in detail in the majority party's caucus. On occasion, the governor appeared in his party's caucus to defend a particularly important item.[15] In states where caucuses are not extensively used, leadership committees are likely to play a major role in managing legislative business. Some states require the standing committees to release all bills to a leadership committee — usually the rules committee — before the end of a session. Other states empower such a committee to take possession of all bills introduced into the chamber after a certain calendar date.

Whatever specific procedures are used, the distribution of political power in state legislatures seems much more uneven than is true of the U. S. Congress. In the part-time state assembly, few legislators other than the leaders are prepared to devote full working time to legislative affairs. A major political resource of the leadership is the skill that grows out of their heavy commitment of time to the legislature's tasks. The politicians constituting the leadership of a state legislature are likely to vary from session to session — one study showed that in only a third of the state legislative chambers did the presiding officer remain for as long as eight years.[16] Thus, a marked difference exists between the transient leaders of a state assembly and the more permanent legislative hierarchy in Congress. But whoever the leaders are in a given session, the directions taken by the state legislature are likely to depend greatly on their particular activities.

So far we have discussed the ways in which state legislatures reveal a lower level of institutionalization than does Congress without touching on what is perhaps the most interesting problem associated with the concept of institutionalization, namely, its causes. In his study of the U. S. House of Representatives, Polsby states that no one is certain of the causes of the process, but he suggests that they are related to the political responsibilities assumed by a particular institution. "As the responsibilities of the national government grew, as a larger proportion of the national economy was affected by decisions taken at the center, the agencies of the national government institutionalized."[17] From the discussion of the state political process in chapters 2 and 3, there is good reason to think that this speculation explains the more informal (less institutionalized) arrangement of state assemblies. The low visibility and nebulousness that traditionally has characterized the politics of the states have permitted many state legislatures to operate in much the same fashion that Congress did in the nineteenth century.

In addition, the way in which state legislators have defined their jobs as legislators has probably contributed to a lack of permanent organization and professionalism in state assemblies. Few legislators seem to perceive responsibility for initiating and making policy as a major part of their work. When a group of Maine state senators and representatives were asked in 1971 about their tasks ("What are the most important things that you do as a state legislator?"), they stressed representing their districts and becoming skillful in the legislative process ahead of the job of developing regional or statewide public policy.[18] On the whole, state legislators seem to be most effective in performing chores for constituents and least successful in overseeing the executive branch to insure that programs adopted by the legislature are properly carried out. As John Pittenger, a part-time college professor and former Pennsylvania legislator, has commented in regard to his state assembly: "If I were grading the legislature, I'd give them a B-plus on constituent homework, a C-plus on the quality of legislation, and a D on legislative oversight."[19]

Reforming the Legislature. But some of these patterns are changing. The new pressures on state government for programs and policy direction have led to a reexamination of the state legislative institution. Every state has in the past decade or so undertaken modification of its existing legislative practices in some way. The general goal has been to make the state assembly a more permanent institutionalized agency in the management of state affairs. As we will note in the next section, the rise of the governor's authority has virtually compelled legislatures to modernize themselves in order to retain a share of power with the executive in the formulation of policy. Three of the most important areas of modification have been reapportionment, compensation, and professional staffing.

Undoubtedly the most important alteration to take place in the 1960s was reapportionment. All state legislatures redrew their district boundaries in the 1960s as a direct consequence of *Baker* v. *Carr* (1962) and later Supreme Court decisions. Reapportionment has had many consequences — not the least of which has been simply the discovery of the state legislature by many citizens who had rarely given the institution much thought. New opportunities for recruiting more active and informed people to legislative service have opened up. The consolidation of many sparsely populated rural districts (under the "one man, one vote" formula) has probably reduced the number of "reluctant" legislators in state assemblies. (In the 1959 study of Connecticut's House, the "reluctant" legislators — men and women who did not wish to serve in the assembly but who were finally talked into doing so — came mainly from rural districts in that very badly apportioned state.) The impact of reapportionment on policy generally has been a more equitable distribution of state aid among rural and urban areas and increased spending in many states in such urban-related areas as education and public health.[20]

To attract a more permanent body of legislators the states have significantly improved salaries. Between 1965 and 1975 the median legislative compensation (per biennium) in the states moved from $7,167 to $18,216.[21] In 1975 twenty states, mostly large urban states, paid their legislators $10,000 per year or more, compared to only three in this category in 1965. Legislative salaries approach those of U. S. congressmen only in the state of California, where in 1974 – 1975 members of the state house and senate earned a total of $32,070 per year plus expenses. Yet the figures for the states generally in the mid-1970s surely represented a major departure from the few-hundred-dollars-a-year idea of legislative compensation that prevailed in some areas ten years earlier. In most states, legislators can now devote at least half their working time to their duties without serious financial loss.

Finally, all state legislatures are beginning to strengthen the state assembly as an institution. In the period between 1960 and 1976 the number of states opting for annual, instead of biennial, sessions increased from nineteen to thirty-six.[22] Importantly, the number of states maintaining an agency for continuous study of revenues and expenditures — a crucial instrument enabling the legislatures to maintain some form of coequality with the executive branch — increased in the 1960 – 1976 period from twenty-five to forty-seven. In states that have long had weak standing committees, staffs are being added to these units. Some states have reduced the number of standing committees to permit legislators to devote more time to areas of specialization. In a number of legislatures the committees are now beginning to work on a year-round basis, outside of the regular legislative sessions as well as during the sessions, in order to study issues, prepare proposals for consideration by the full chambers, and oversee the executive branch. A positive sign is that the states are not likely to follow the model of the U. S. House and become so bureaucratized — in the sense that power is heavily concentrated in specialized committees — that they have trouble responding to contemporary needs. Indeed, the national legislature presently seems more inclined to follow the model of state assemblies in providing controls on its own standing committees. Democratic chairmen of standing committees in the U. S. House of Representatives must — under rules adopted in the early 1970s — be approved by the full Democratic caucus before they can assume their positions. This weakens the seniority system in Washington. Such changes suggest that in future years state legislatures and the Congress may resemble each other more fully than in the past, especially in terms of the internal distribution of power.

The Problem of State Administration

Much as the politics of states have produced significant differences in state legislatures as compared to the U. S. Congress, so, too, have these patterns made the office of governor different from that of the president. Certain parallels exist, of course. Both national and state constitutions assign the presidency and the governorship the formal duties of executing public policy. Because each office is held by one individual, it is more visible to most citizens than are the collegially structured legislatures and courts. And governors and presidents can generally make the strongest claim to speak for the "public interest" in their respective constituencies, inasmuch as they each have the broadest electoral base. Yet, "the governor is not a little President."[23] The states have traditionally been reluctant to equip their governors with the kinds of formal legal powers that the president has long possessed in national affairs. Or, to put it another way, the offices of governors and state administrators have long faced the same problem of institutional amorphousness that has afflicted state legislatures.

Three Values in Administration. What are the structural weaknesses of the contemporary governorship? A good general answer to this question was provided by Herbert Kaufman. Kaufman maintains that three basic political values have guided architects of state government since the American Revolution. The three values he finds crucial are representativeness, neutral competence, and executive leadership.[24] Although one value has tended to predominate over the others at particular periods in history, all three can be seen at work today in the organization of the typical state's executive branch. Two of the values, representativeness and neutral competence, specifically and significantly detract from the governor's capacity to direct state affairs.

The notion of *representativeness* refers to a belief shared by citizens that state officials making decisions affecting them should be subject to popular election. This value was dominant in state governments until the Civil War. In the early 1800s, as the states began to add new departments and functions, they made the officials in charge of these agencies popularly elected. The notion of representativeness fell out of favor after the Civil War, because of abuses by political machines in the states and corruption in some state legislatures. But nearly all the states continue at present to elect some subordinate officials in their executive branches. In the great majority of states, for instance, the offices of attorney general, secretary of state, and treasurer are filled by statewide election. Only New Jersey, Maine, New Hampshire, Tennessee, Alaska, and Hawaii do not elect at least one of these officials by popular ballot.

The concept of *neutral competence* replaced representativeness as the prevailing value in the latter part of the nineteenth century. Neutral competence implies that state officials should have training and expertise for the jobs they perform and that governmental decisions should be based on professional, not partisan, considerations.[25] Instead of relying on popular elections to fill state offices, the states began to create numerous boards and commissions and to lodge administrative power with them. The governor's authority to name the members of these boards was bound with various restrictions: the states often required the boards to have bipartisan memberships; the terms of the commissioners frequently exceeded those of the governor himself; and the members of the boards could not be removed unless legal charges were brought against them.

The goal of all this was to take a great part of the administration of state affairs "out of politics" and to turn it over to various technical experts. The popularity of neutral competence waned in the early decades of the twentieth century. The states found that the proliferation of independent agencies and commissions made administrative co-ordination of public programs almost unattainable. Even worse, it was nearly impossible for voters or their elected representatives, such as legislators or governors, to hold state administrations responsible for the conduct of public affairs. Today, however, the idea of neutral competence is still clearly reflected in the administrative organizations of some states. In Oklahoma as of 1974, for instance, the heads of thirteen functional departments, including those responsible for highways, health, human resources, conservation, and public assistance, were still chosen by independent boards and commissions. In South Carolina in the same year, some eleven agency heads received their appointments through boards or commissions largely independent of the governor.[26]

The third value, *executive leadership*, reflects the belief that state governmental decisions should be centrally coordinated. It stresses the need for coherent management of public policy and recommends that responsibility for state affairs be assigned to one or two top public officials. This idea has generally prevailed in state administrative reorganizations since World War I. Beginning with the Illinois reorganization under Governor Frank Lowden in 1917, the states have gradually equipped governors with additional powers over their administrative families. Typical reforms have included lengthening governors' terms of office (usually from two to four years), permitting them to succeed themselves in office, assigning to them the primary responsibility for formulating the state budget, and specifying that the heads of major departments may serve only at the governor's pleasure. Yet, as the cases of Oklahoma and South Carolina suggest, the states have not uniformly committed themselves to the idea of executive leadership. In most, the governor still lags well behind the president in his formal administrative power.

The fact that all three values — representativeness, neutral competence, and executive leadership — can be seen at work today invites us to consider the politics of state administration. The most general cause for the failure of states to reform their executive branches has been low visibility. For many citizens, state government is a remote, dimly perceived set of activities that comes into view — if at all — only during exciting gubernatorial campaigns or moments of crisis. As noted in chapter 1, states have differed from many large American cities in that the states have not witnessed the emergence of broadly based coalitions of voters intent on demanding specific kinds of services and policies. Public demand for strong executive leadership has thus been missing in many states. But there are additional causes for the failure to strengthen the executive. In every state certain of the most involved and informed groups in state politics have a vested interest in keeping administrative power fragmented and out of the hands of the governor. Thus the notions of representativeness and neutral competence continue as viable guidelines in organizing present-day state government because they serve the needs of some identifiable groups in state politics.

Opponents of Executive Leadership. Three political groups interested in preventing strong executive coordination can be identified. One is composed of interest groups whose activities are closely regulated by certain state agencies. Such groups generally believe that their power over decisions affecting them is enhanced if the agency in question is kept independent of the governor. Education groups want a say in the naming of the head of the state department of education, perhaps through his or her appointment by a state board of education on which they hold seats.[27] In this way, they argue, education can be "kept out of state politics." Sports enthusiasts insist that the state fish and game commission be responsive to their needs only, and they thus seek to keep that unit outside of the governor's control. Automobile groups think that the state's motor-fuels taxes should be used exclusively for road construction and maintenance. For this reason they try to ensure the segregation of monies from the governor's general fund. Such separatist pressures are felt at every level of government, but they seem to be especially influential in state politics, where there are fewer countervailing forces urging integration and coordination of public functions in the name of some broader "general interest."

A second group that often supports the idea of a loosely organized state executive consists of career professionals in certain state departments. There is reason to believe that "professionalism . . . produces particularly strong tendencies toward separatism."[28] Professionals, equipped as they are with extensive technical knowledge, usually want their agencies to remain independent of gubernatorial control. They often claim that placing their agency's functions under the governor's direct supervision will lead to "political interference" in its activities and thus to a reduction in effective service to its clients. The middleman role of the states in the federal system probably reinforces this desire for independence. Career people in state agencies generally deal extensively with both federal and local agency counterparts. In terms of federal policies, state bureaucrats tend to prefer the grants-in-aid approach under which federal funds come to their individual departments, while governors strongly favor the idea of revenue sharing, that is, the allocation of federal funds to the states largely without strings. An additional separatist tendency is shown by the existence of interstate organizations of state departmental officials. State executives in the areas of public works, health, and natural resources in particular seem to have strong national organizations and to reflect a degree of independence from their governors because of these close interstate ties.[29]

A third group that often opposes a fully integrated state administration consists of state legislators. Part of their reluctance can be attributed to the institutional rivalry between executive and legislative branches that has existed since the first encounters of the medieval British parliaments with the British Crown. But a larger part of the problem comes from the state legislature's own weaknesses, or its lack of institutionalization. Whatever difficulties governors face in managing their administrative families, they at least are fulltime officials; state legislators in many areas have not yet reached that stage. Historically, the state legislature has been poorly equipped to engage in careful surveillance of the state executive branch. This has been particularly true with respect to securing information on various programs and policies that the governor has the tools to acquire. The legislatures' traditional solution to this problem has been to keep portions of the state administration legally out of the governor's hands and, usually, in those of the legislature. When a sample of 933 state executives were asked in the 1960s who exercised greater control over their agencies' affairs, 44 percent named the legislature as having more power, and 32 percent indicated that the governor had the most influence.[30]

With interest groups, career state employees, and state legislators joining hands to restrict the governor's power, it is little wonder that representativeness and neutral competence continue to hold sway in many states. Although the notion of executive leadership has prevailed on a national basis since World War I, the mix of representativeness, neutral competence, and executive leadership in individual states varies enormously. It may be helpful at this point to look at the governor's power in state politics on a comparative basis.

In the late 1960s Joseph A. Schlesinger rated the governor's power in each state according to four broad indexes — tenure potential, extent of appointive powers, budgetary authority, and veto power.[31] The states revealed wide diversity. In some states the governor was limited to four years in office; in others there were no legal restraints on reelection. In some states he was surrounded by cabinet officers who were either elected or appointed by a group of which he was not a member; in other states the governor could name the officials heading the major state departments. In some states budgetary and veto powers were extensive; in other states they were practically nonexistent. Schlesinger found that the following states granted most complete authority to the governor over the executive branch: New York, Illinois, Hawaii, California, Michigan, Minnesota, New Jersey, Pennsylvania, and Maryland. States having the weakest governors in terms of formal power were Texas, West Virginia, South Carolina, Florida, Indiana, Mississippi, North Carolina, and New Mexico.

The most obvious factor associated with the formal strength of governors is the size of their states. The thirteen states having the highest rating for their governors accounted in 1960 for 52 percent of the total U. S. population. The diversity and complexity of these large states have made it necessary for them to equip their governors with a good deal of formal legal power. Most resembling the nation as a whole in their social heterogeneity, these states most approximate the federal executive in their assignment of administrative authority to their governors. A second factor related to differences in the formal powers of state governors is the degree of party competition in their states. Texas, a large state that has a relatively weak governor, is a one-party state; in fact, it is the only one of the seven largest states to have a one-party system. Conversely, Wyoming and Utah, sparsely populated states having relatively strong governors, have had closely competitive political parties. Parties in a competitive situation generally find that a powerful governor's office contributes toward their making a mark in state politics.

The analysis here should not be taken to mean that governors in small rural states necessarily have less total power than governors in large well-populated states. Governors in New Mexico and Mississippi may have as much political influence within their states as do governors in New York or Illinois, even though the governor's office is legally much weaker in the first two states. In a small state a governor's personal appeal and skill in bargaining may well compensate for deficiencies in the formal legal powers of the office.[32]

It seems safe to say that all governors are more dependent on the informal resources of bargaining, persuasion, and publicity than is the president. Most scholars think that governors must rely far too heavily on these resources. In an administratively fragmented state, the governor may devote much time to personal negotiations not with other politicians but with private citizens. A study detailing the visits made to the office of a governor of Arkansas found that 48 percent of the calls (in terms of the portion of the governor's time consumed) dealt with personal requests made by private citizens.[33] Unlike the president, whose control over administrative machinery affords him the opportunity to line up political support on the basis of broad programs, the governor may find that dealings with private citizens constitute a necessary means of building an effective political base. When a governor is forced to act in this way, the power of the governorship in a state's political system tends to fluctuate. Terry Sanford, former governor of North Carolina, has observed that:

> We often see a strong governor in a state followed by a weak or ineffective one. The strength of a governor must too often rest in personality or public appeal, or force of conviction, or emergencies which coalesce support for needed action. His achievement too often is personal and not, as in the Presidency, that of his executive office and its supporting institutions.[34]

Governors, Legislators, and Bureaucrats

The structural problem of state administration invites us to consider the interaction between the governor and other state officials (legislators and bureaucrats) in the making and carrying out of state policy. The thrust of this section is that governors are more effective as policy formulators — at least they are better equipped to perform that role — than they are implementors of policy. This imbalance is partly due to the fragmentation of the state executive branch. But as we will note here, the pattern also has roots in the politics of the states. The states seem to have provided governors with established (or institutionalized) powers in policy formulation even as they have often made it difficult for them to execute programs once these have been authorized.

The Governor's Power in Policy Formation. The nature of the relationship between the governor and state legislators is a key to the governor's power to formulate policy. Under the state constitution, the legislature is responsible for the making of law. As a "chief legislator," a governor can greatly affect the policy-making process. Governors in all the states enjoy several legal powers permitting them a significant impact on legislative affairs. First, most states assign to the governor the task of preparing and submitting to the legislature the state budget. It is hard to overestimate the importance of the budget in shaping the debates and maneuvers in a legislative session. State assemblies usually have trouble getting started until they see the governor's budget requests. Once these have finally cleared the legislative process, usually many months later, the legislature is normally ready to adjourn. Whatever the imposing technicalities of budget recommendations, legislators recognize spending requests as "the most authoritative single measure of what the executive's program actually is."[35] Examining the governor's budget can indicate whether a campaign promise will become a reality. A second significant power of the chief executive is the calling of special legislative sessions. Because state legislatures meet less often than does Congress, some of their most critical work occasionally occurs in special sessions. In three-fifths of the states the governor constitutionally possesses the sole power to call special sessions of the legislature. Further, in one-third of the states he can set the agenda for the special session. A third gubernatorial control is the executive veto. Governors in forty-two states possess an item veto, which permits the chief executive to excise a small part of the bill, usually an appropria- tions measure, before signing the total bill into law. The threat of the item veto is often a useful tool in winning legislative support for the governor's policy ideas. Executive vetoes are almost never overridden in most states.[36]

Apart from legal powers, the governor has certain political ad- vantages in negotiating policy with the state legislature. One is that nearly all governors are experienced office holders while few state legislators can claim much previous political training. Of the 156 governors who served in the 1960s, all but 11 had held prior public office.[37] A common career route followed by a prospective governor is to begin public service as a state legislator or as a law enforcement officer and later to hold a statewide administrative office (especially the post of lieutenant governor or attorney general). About half the gov- ernors in the 1960s had this kind of background. In contrast, about half the members of state legislatures enter public service for the first time as legislators and many of these regard themselves as citizen legislators who intend to serve only a single term of office. The governor's personal skills are buttressed by the presence of a professional office staff. A survey of forty states indicated that the typical governor was served by seven professional persons, including legislative assistants and policy researchers, and this report did not include several large states where staff numbers are presumably greater.[38] A shortage of staff assistance in state legislatures has, of course, made it difficult for members of state assemblies to counter the governor's proposals with their own.

A governor's relationships with members of the state legislature obviously depend on the political circumstances of individual states. In certain southern states, namely, Kentucky, Alabama, and Georgia, the governor traditionally has been able to name the house and senate floor leaders.[39] Other state legislatures insist on developing their own leadership. The governor's leadership of his political party is usually an advantage in those states with strong party organizations (mainly the individualistic states). If a basis for party cohesion already exists, the governor can mobilize the resources of the legislative party behind his programs. On the other hand, governors frequently face legislatures controlled by the opposition party and find they must mute partisan appeals. In a state where political parties are weak or loosely organized, a chief executive may discover that settling intraparty squabbles consumes a substantial portion of his time. Overall, the ability of the governor to use his legislative party for program purposes seems to depend mainly on his political reputation in the state as a whole. An interesting study of the success of governors in securing legislative support for their proposals (covering thirty-four states for the period from 1946 to 1960) found that a governor who achieved high success in a particular legislative session typically ran very strongly in the gubernatorial primary following the legislative session.[40] Legislators in these states apparently were responding — in their decisions to support the chief executive — to their assessment of his future staying power in state politics.

Of course, a governor must define his job in activist terms to be effective in the task of formulating public policy. If a chief executive regards his position as that of an overseer, or shies away from conflict, or develops a reputation for backing down in a crisis, other politicians may doubt his willingness to follow through on his policy aims. But where a governor shows a strong willingness to persist in a plan of action and to take risks, his imprint on the policies of his state can be large. During the 1960s, Governor Nelson Rockefeller of New York combined the legal and political powers of his office with substantial personal leadership to raise the level of spending in his state. In the same decade Governor Ronald Reagan of California mobilized similar resources to curb the growth of programs in his state.[41]

An indication of the importance of policy formulation in the work of the state chief executive is the amount of time he devotes to formulating policy. Accounting for one month's schedule of an Illinois governor, a researcher noted that some 54 percent of that governor's time was devoted to the functions of public relations, legislative affairs, and political leadership.[42] The Illinois governor appeared to spend only about 20 percent of his working hours on strictly management problems, as measured by his meetings with state administrative officials, conferences with his personal staff on administrative problems, and the like. Governors seem historically to have found that they can best make their mark on state affairs by proposing and developing programs, with an eye toward reelection or perhaps toward a race for the U. S. Senate. A host of factors, including the traditional fragmentation of state administration and the middle position of the states in the federal system, have made commitments of gubernatorial energy to the tasks of policy execution simply less attractive.

The Governor's New Concern with Administration. Present-day developments in state affairs, however, suggest a growing importance of administrative concerns. Indeed, certain headline issues of state politics of the mid-1970s fall into that category. One event is the growth of public employee unions and concomitant demands for collective bargaining rights for state workers. As of 1975 some 210,000 state employees were members of the American Federation of State, County, and Municipal Employees, an AFL-CIO affiliate.[43] In New York and California, over 90 percent of state workers are members of union organizations. The rise of public unions raises questions of the scope of collective bargaining and the right of employees in state administrations to strike. A second management issue is finance. All states currently need to reexamine their tax structures and especially their spending programs as a consequence of continued economic uncertainty. In early 1975 several governors were forecasting deficits in their state budgets. In a period of sharply limited resources, the states are struggling to make their management of programs more dependable and effective.

Events will probably accelerate existing trends toward improved administrative structures for the states. As we noted in the previous section, the idea of "executive leadership" has been uppermost in the minds of state reformers since the second decade of this century, but progress toward its fulfillment has been exceedingly slow. Some quickening nevertheless did occur in the late 1960s and the 1970s in response to generalized efforts to strengthen state institutions. Since 1970 eight states have extended the governor's term from two years to four years (bringing to forty-seven the number of states in 1976 having a four-year gubernatorial term). Since 1970 Indiana and West Virginia have dropped their prohibitions against a governor succeeding himself (bringing to forty-two the number of states in 1976 permitting a governor to serve at least two terms of office). Apart from lengthening the governor's term, and thereby strengthening his hand in the management of state affairs, several states have consolidated scattered boards and commissions into a few major departments. About one-third of the states adopted some form of state administrative reorganization between 1966 and 1974.[44] Though these provisions did not automatically increase the governor's authority, they did provide for greater integration of the executive branch and for more independence of the executive establishment from the state legislature. One interesting power that governors have started to acquire is the authority to reorganize the executive branch by executive order, that is, by the governor's own decision. This move is subject only to a legislative veto. As of 1972 thirteen states had equipped their chief executives with reorganization powers.

In the crucial areas of financial and personnel control, the governor's power has also been slowly growing. Forty-two states in 1976 had departments of finance and administration, compared with twenty-eight states a decade earlier.[45] A department of finance and administration combines many central service functions along with finance, such as budgeting, purchasing, and accounting. In all but one state with such a department, the governor nominates its head, and in seventeen states the governor alone is responsible for this appointment. In most states these departments are centers for development of new budget systems emphasizing program evaluation. In the personnel field, forty-eight states now have departments of personnel in comparison with the forty-two states which had such agencies in 1966. The governor is involved in the appointment of the personnel director in twenty-five of the states. Historically, the rise of the merit system in state government led to a complete separation of the personnel function from the governor's hands in order to minimize the influence of party politics on personnel decisions. A recent trend, however, has been to integrate personnel activities with line officials (officials who administer programs) and to bring personnel activities under the chief executive's authority. The states usually retain their civil service commissions or personnel boards — which once had substantial administrative functions — for appeals and for certain rule-making functions.[46]

The governor's formal powers are important in helping him to shape the work of individual administrative departments. A study of the budget requests of state agencies in nineteen states found that the governor's budget recommendation was normally a crucial ingredient in determining what appropriation an administrative agency finally received from the state legislature.[47] Governors typically pared down agency requests to conform to their own budget plans, and the legislatures usually — though not always — followed the governors' lead. Of significance to our discussion is that those governors who had the greatest success in securing approval for their recommendations in the legislature were chief executives who could be reelected and who had broad appointive powers. In cases where a governor was surrounded by many officials over whom he had little control, administrative agencies were inclined to deal directly with the legislature. In these instances the governor's own recommendations were more apt to be modified or ignored. Formal administrative powers appear, in other words, to count in the governor's political relationships.

The extent to which the states equip their governors with genuine administrative power in coming years will probably depend on intensity of management-type issues in the states and also on the speed of legislative reform. As we have seen, the state legislature has often been at the forefront in opposing the notion of placing independent agencies under the direct control of the governor. Possibly in recognition of their weakness — relative to the governor — in the job of policy formulation, legislators have sought instead to take a hand in policy execution by maintaining supervisory controls over various administrative agencies. But state legislatures are steadily improving their operations. As they become more institutionalized, their opposition to executive integration may recede and the executive branch too may develop more coherence. Under that pattern, the separation of powers system would work at the state level in a manner more closely resembling the national arrangement.

State Courts

The central argument up to this point has been that the relatively amorphous, unsystematic character of U. S. state politics has led state legislatures and executives until recently to show few professional and bureaucratic tendencies. State courts have been the least carefully studied agency in state politics. Only in the past fifteen years have researchers tried explicitly to look at them as political forces rather than as neutral arbiters of the law. Courts are involved no less than legislatures and executives in the task of setting policies for the states. Thus courts in the states should reveal — if our analysis has been correct — patterns similar to those of legislatures, governors, and bureaucracies.

The Structure of State Courts. Before the politics of state courts are considered, it is important to note briefly the general structure of state courts. The states correspond to the federal judicial pattern in that they generally employ a hierarchical system of three levels of courts. But state court systems are more weighted toward the trial level than is the federal judicial hierarchy. The federal structure has only one level of trial courts (federal district courts) and two levels of appellate courts (federal circuit courts of appeals and the U. S. Supreme Court). The states typically have two distinct layers of trial courts and one level of appellate courts. This difference is mainly due to the much greater volume of judicial business that the states are required to handle. (The overwhelming bulk of domestic law with which citizens come into daily contact consists of state and local statutes and ordinances, not federal laws.) Additionally, the states tend to use a variety of specialized trial courts — the more populous the state, usually, the more of these courts — whose nomenclature unfortunately invites considerable confusion. Still, in each state three distinct levels of courts are visible.

Every state has, at the base of its judicial hierarchy, a layer of courts designed to handle violations of civil and criminal law of a minor character.[48] The various names of these courts are familiar: justice-of-the-peace courts, magistrate courts, municipal courts, traffic courts, and, in some states, district courts. These "petty" trial courts exhibit two main characteristics. First, their jurisdiction is limited to minor cases. In most states they cannot hear civil cases involving more than a thousand dollars, and they cannot usually take criminal cases for which the maximum jail sentence exceeds one year. Second, these courts are not generally courts of record. That is, they do not usually keep a formal transcript of their proceedings. Their procedure is usually "summary and informal" and only the names of the parties, their attorneys, and the judge's decision are recorded.[49] A citizen who loses a case in this type of court normally has a right of appeal to a higher trial court.

A second layer of courts in all states consists of trial courts of general jurisdiction. These are courts of record. Although they do occasionally retry cases appealed to them from the "petty" courts, their main function is to act as courts of first instance for the serious civil and criminal cases that "petty" courts are not permitted to handle. Again, a galaxy of names is associated with these courts: in different states they are called superior courts, courts of common pleas, district courts, county courts, and circuit courts. The states generally divide themselves into judicial districts and assign one of these courts to each geographical area. In densely populated areas, there may be several judges presiding over the particular trial court. And the more populous states usually employ several specialized courts at this level. Typical of these are courts of quarter sessions (criminal cases only), surrogates courts (wills and estates), and divorce and family relations courts.

Finally, every state has at least one appeals court. In twenty-six states, there is only one court of last resort, variously called the supreme court, the supreme judicial court, the court of appeals, or the supreme court of errors. Its primary function is to review decisions made in trial courts. Except in unusual circumstances, these courts do not deal with the facts of a case; they are concerned only with the accuracy with which the lower court interpreted and applied the law in a specific case. About half the states (twenty-four) provide, in addition to their court of last resort, an intermediate appeals court. This unit also hears appeals from trial courts. Although in some states it may have a fairly specialized jurisdiction (for instance, it may hear all appeals in cases growing out of state regulatory agencies), its general function is to assist the highest court. Because every state affords its litigants the right of at least one appeal from the trial court level, in larger states the single court of last resort is not able to handle all appeals directly and needs the assistance of an intermediate court.

The Politics of State Courts. This is only the barest outline of the structure of state courts, but it is sufficient for us to begin looking at their politics. Our discussion deals with two problems: first, how court systems as a whole reflect the process of state politics, and second, how supreme courts in the states respond to the politics of their particular state.

So far as judicial structures in the states are concerned, the rather neat hierarchical appearance of the usual state court system is misleading. The links between courts of last resort (supreme courts) and trial courts are a good deal more tenuous and sporadic than an organization chart would suggest. Although the states permit cases decided in their trial courts at least one appeal to a higher court, most cases terminate at the trial court level. As one observer has put it: "For most practical purposes, the local trial court is *both* the [U. S.] Supreme Court and the state's court of last resort."[50] A study of 388 noncriminal cases settled by one urban trial court in New York found that less than one-fourth were later heard by the New York appellate courts. Many of these 388 cases involved significant questions of public policy, especially in the field of land use and zoning. In only 7 percent of all the cases was the decision of the trial court ultimately reversed at the appeals level. Contrary to long-standing assumptions that trial courts deal only in routine, largely private law matters, recent analysis indicates that the policy-making functions of trial courts are nearly equal to those of higher tribunals.

The importance of the decisions of trial courts is heightened by the fact that, in most states, these courts are closely tied to political groups in the districts where they sit. Trial judges are popularly elected in thirty-two states, and even where they are appointed (normally by the governor) local political leaders usually have a voice in their selection. For a county political party, especially in an urban county, control over the local court system constitutes a major political prize. Judges often have considerable patronage powers covering not only clerkships and other court positions but extending to the often lucrative jobs of trustee, appraiser of estates, and receiver in bankruptcy. That judges are influenced in these appointments by the party that helped them win their office is attested to in a comment of a New York trial judge:

> In making many of these appointments most judges I know, including myself, accept and recognize recommendations from the party of their affiliation. They require that the person to be designated be honest and competent. Judges will also appoint friends on the same basis, and encourage deserving young lawyers by thus recognizing them.[51]

The impact that the local political structure has on the judges' handling of cases is difficult to measure, although a considerable amount of influence doubtless exists. At the "petty" court level, justices of the peace (J.P.s) long ago won the cynical nickname of "justice for the plaintiff" — in part because of their propensity to decide traffic cases that pit local police against passing motorists, notably motorists residing outside of the J.P.'s district, in favor of the local police. Local politics also seem to intrude into decisions made in trial courts of general jurisdiction. In a study of the cases decided in one such trial court, Kenneth Dolbeare found that citizens unhappy with local zoning ordinances had a better chance of successfully challenging them when their attorney was part of a law firm with a member in county public office than when their attorney came from a nonpolitical firm. And if the public officeholder from the law firm was of the same political party as the judge, chances of winning were somewhat higher than if he or she were of the opposing party.[52]

The point here is that state trial courts are tied to the political process, and the politics with which they are associated tend to be distinctly local politics, not statewide politics. Although state supreme courts are equipped with both a reviewing power and a power to command lower tribunals to take certain actions (for instance, to grant a change of venue in a trial), the highest courts exercise nothing like day-to-day supervision over their local courts. Viewed as a whole, the typical state court system has a fairly low degree of institutionalization. In this respect it is comparable to the structure of state legislatures and state executives. For state judiciaries the problem of coordination is an especially old one. One specialist has noted that "in 1950 state courts had about the same structure and powers that they had one hundred years before."[53] The cause of this problem has been political. The nebulous quality of state politics as such has reinforced the attachments of local courts to local areas. In order for state supreme courts to exercise the kind of meaningful control over lower courts that a formal bureaucratic model would suggest, political power in the states would have to be much more fully centralized in the hands of the state government than it typically has been.

In the past decade political scientists have paid particular attention to state supreme courts as articulators of public policy. In light of the fact that the Constitution (according to Article VI) is the supreme law of the land and that state judges are bound thereby, interest has focused on the role of state judges in enforcing national constitutional norms. What decisions do state supreme court judges make when national policy and state norms conflict? This question raises the more basic issue of the extent to which state supreme courts themselves respond to variations in state politics.

Evidence suggests that courts of last resort in the states vary in their decision-making activities according to the vagaries of state politics, but they do so less than state executives and state legislatures. In a national study of the voting behavior of judges in courts of last resort, one student found marked differences between Republican and Democratic judges in their decisions in a number of areas. Democratic judges sitting on the same supreme courts with Republican judges were more prone to favor "the defense in criminal cases, the administrative agency in business regulation cases . . . , the claimant in unemployment compensation cases . . . , the tenant in landlord-tenant cases, the labor union in labor-management cases, and the debtor in creditor-debtor cases."[54] These differences do not mean that judges consciously attempt to follow a party line in their work. More likely, they rely on personal standards and these standards frequently account for their political party affiliation.[55]

Dissent in the highest state courts also occurs, of course, when the courts are controlled by members of the same political party. A recent study of the highest courts in all fifty states from 1961 to 1967 found that judges on the top state benches dissented, on a nationwide average, in 13.5 percent of the decisions they handed down.[56] Generally, rates of dissent here were correlated with the social heterogeneity of the states and, somewhat more modestly, with the variable of political party competition. States with a high level of urbanism and social diversity, and with strongly competitive party systems, revealed more dissent among their top judges than states without these characteristics. Judges in large urban states, especially, showed a tendency to dissent in cases

involving intergovernmental relations and the powers and responsibilities of governmental offices. In these states, rural-urban and
interurban legal conflicts were apparently the most intense.

Some connection does exist, then, between the decision-making
behavior of the highest state courts and the politics peculiar to the areas
they serve. However, the relationships tend to be modest ones. In the
study just discussed, the authors note that the limited association among
state political characteristics and the rate of dissent in the highest courts
they studied imply that on-bench, working relationships among the
judges "have a significant role in the determination of dissent rates in
state supreme courts."[57] These internal relationships are probably
important in shaping the decisions of the courts because the highest
courts in the states are insulated from political pressures — certainly
more so than state executive and legislative bodies. For one thing,
although judges of the highest court are popularly elected in twenty-five
states (on a partisan ballot in thirteen states and on a nonpartisan ballot
in twelve), their terms of office are much longer than those of legislators
and governors. Terms of judges sitting on courts of last resort are not
less than six years in any state and extend to life tenure in New Jersey
and Rhode Island and to age seventy in New Hampshire and Massachusetts. Furthermore, the style of judicial decision making differs significantly from executive and legislative decision making.[58] The courts are
protected by a veritable maze of technical procedures. Access to the
highest courts is usually limited to persons who can retain counsel and
who are themselves involved in a genuine case or controversy (not
merely a theoretical problem) over which the court has jurisdiction.

Judges are also insulated by the manner in which they attain their
positions. A survey of 441 judges of the highest courts indicated that
over three quarters of them were elevated to the top state bench from
the position of trial judge or appellate court judge.[59] Most judges begin
their careers as local prosecutors or as state legislators, and move from
those positions into a trial judgeship. The hierarchy of offices followed
by judges of the highest courts is tighter than that pursued by members
of other state agencies. For instance, senior state administrators tend to
be experienced in a wide variety of offices and to more frequently have
resided in other states.[60]

The greater insulation of state supreme courts, compared to other
decision-making agencies in state politics, is suggested in a study of
eleven southern state courts of last resort for the period from 1954 to
1963.[61] The investigation covered a total of 198 civil rights cases decided
by these courts in that period. Blacks (who were either plaintiff or
defendant in all cases) won favorable verdicts in about one-third of the
decisions. This is a strikingly liberal record on the part of top southern

judges in these years, given the almost unanimous hostility to the U. S. Supreme Court's *Brown* v. *Board of Education* decision voiced by southern politicians during the same period. The highest courts in the states of the South seemed to be far more receptive to black demands than did the state trial courts. Of the forty-five cases in which one of the eleven highest courts reversed a decision of a state trial court, 94 percent were won by black litigants in the court of last resort after having lost their cases at the trial court level. The political environment of the states shapes and molds the operation of all state institutions, but the highest state courts still maintain a considerable degree of independence in their work. At the present time, it does not appear that the political processes in individual states — different as these processes are — significantly impede state supreme court judges from enforcing the U. S. Constitution.

Judicial Policy Making. How do state judges perceive their role as policy makers? Most judges seem to view their fundamental responsibility as interpreting the law, not writing new law. A survey of judges of the courts of last resort in the states of New Jersey, Louisiana, Pennsylvania, and Massachusetts found that 53 percent of the judges on these benches regarded themselves as law interpreters while 23 percent saw their role primarily as that of lawmaker.[62] The remaining judges mostly perceived themselves as "pragmatists," meaning that they combined elements of the law-interpreting and lawmaking roles in their work and tried to match their settlement of a case to the special issues and circumstances surrounding it. A study of judges sitting on highest court benches in Maryland, New York, Virginia, and Delaware resulted in similar findings: twelve of these judges took a law-interpreter view of their responsibilities, only three seemed to hold to the lawmaker role, and seven judges took an eclectic view of their work.[63] The conservatism of state judges in role perception is reflected in some policy areas. For instance, state courts have for the most part been reluctant to expand the rights of criminal defendants. They have generally taken a cautious view of liberal U. S. Supreme Court decisions in this area, and have been slow to apply the rules and philosophy of these decisions to problems in their own states.[64]

On the other hand, state courts can and occasionally do hand down innovative decisions of major significance in the conduct of state affairs. One controversy currently raging in the states involves the method of financing local schools. Most monies for primary and secondary schools are raised through local property taxes. The states try to reduce disparities between rich and poor school districts by furnishing supplemental funds to poorer jurisdictions, but in many areas the quality of education still depends on where a pupil lives and the wealth of his school district. In *Serrano* v. *Priest* (1971), the California Supreme Court declared unconstitutional this type of funding system, holding that it violated the equal protection clause of the Fourteenth Amendment.[65] The impact of the *Serrano* decision may have been more important politically than legally: in a nearly identical case in Texas, the U. S. Supreme Court refused to uphold unconstitutional school funding arrangements based on local property taxes, even though economic disparities existed among school districts. However, the spirit of the *Serrano* decision was reflected in the educational programs of some liberal governors in the early 1970s. In the 1973 Maine legislative session, Governor Kenneth M. Curtis — partly under the impetus of the *Serrano* case — was able to win approval of a new school finance law. A key element was a statewide property tax arrangement. Each school district in Maine now contributes tax dollars according to its total property valuation and receives allocations in accordance with pupil enrollments. An equivalent amount of resources per pupil is thus made available to every district.

Reforms in the Courts. Over the past several years the states have been as interested in improving the operation of their court systems as they have been in reforming their executive and legislative bodies. As with the other two branches, the states have sought to increase the professionalism and the coordination of their courts. In particular, they have tried to make local and trial courts — the heart of the state judiciary — less dependent on the politics of very small areas within the states and more responsive to the rules and policies of the states' highest courts. We may note certain general trends in this field.

First, a number of states have done away with the office of justice of the peace and have placed its functions with courts serving wider geographical areas. Maine, for instance, instituted in 1961 a system of thirteen district courts, each staffed by a full-time judge, to replace its former municipal and peace courts presided over part-time by more than 100 individuals. The objective is not to remove "petty" courts from politics but to make them more politically accountable and visible, both to the people they serve and to the upper levels of the state judiciary. A greater uniformity in the administration of justice is a central goal in these efforts.

In addition, a number of states have provided their court of last resort with new management tools with which to oversee the activities of lower courts. Forty-eight states now employ court administrative officers who collect detailed information on workloads of all state courts and assist in the supervision of judicial budgets and personnel. These officials generally work closely with the chief judge of the state supreme court. In some states, the chief judge is empowered to reassign lower court judges temporarily to hear cases in jurisdictions with heavy case backlogs.

A third reform effort is the use of a Judicial Qualification Commission in the states to maintain professional standards among judges. The function of such a commission is to investigate complaints of incompetence or misconduct concerning individual state judges and to recommend action. After California established its commission in 1961, the unit found it necessary to investigate in depth about one complaint for each five received. Of these, about 40 percent resulted in the removal or resignation of the judge in question.[66] Judicial qualification commissions also work in close collaboration with the state's court of last resort, and the high court normally makes the final determination.

A serious problem facing state courts in the 1970s is that of growing workloads. Many state courts are becoming overburdened because of important changes in our society: a long-term increase in the crime rate, a greater willingness of citizens to use courts to settle both private and public grievances, and a steady expansion of state and local governmental functions that create disputes before courts. The pressure of increased responsibility should provoke continued reform of state judiciaries. At the beginning of this chapter we noted that a key cause for the institutionalization or professionalization of political units is a rise in the demands made on them. As state courts seek assistance from legislatures and other state political groups in improving their function, the judiciary should become more visible to state electorates as well as more systematic in its organization.

Summary

This chapter has examined four arenas of state decision-making — legislatures, governorships, bureaucracies, and courts — with the goal of explaining how each agency responds to demands placed on it and what modifications are occurring in its operations. While the reform tendencies currently at work in these agencies differ in structural terms, the modernization efforts do have this much in common: citizens and politicians are striving to make state decision-making institutions more independent of particularistic or immediate political environments.

For many years significant amounts of the formal decision-making power in state political systems have been legally parceled out to small constituencies who took the greatest interest in state affairs. Private interest groups have long controlled key administrative agencies in the executive branch. Local politicians have often dominated major parts of state court systems. Rural groups for many decades held sway in the state legislature. The process of institutionalization of the decision-making structures of the states can be seen as a process designed to make — however gradually — these agencies more fully responsive to a state's total political environment, and so to resolve the increased demands emanating from it. The implications this process has had, and will have, for public policy making in the states is a topic of the next chapter.

NOTES

1. Alexander Heard, ed., *State Legislatures in American Politics* (Englewood Cliffs, N.J.: Prentice-Hall, 1966), p. 1.
2. Nelson Polsby, "The Institutionalization of the U.S. House of Representatives," *American Political Science Review*, 62 (March 1968), 144–168.
3. Ibid., pp. 148–149.
4. Ibid.
5. Ibid., pp. 154–156.
6. Ibid., p. 156.
7. Charles S. Hyneman, "Tenure and Turnover of Legislative Personnel," *Annals of the American Academy of Political and Social Science*, 195 (1938), 23.
8. Alan Rosenthal, "Turnover in State Legislatures," *American Journal of Political Science*, 18, No. 3 (August 1974), 609–616.
9. David Ray, "Membership Stability in Three State Legislatures: 1893–1969," *American Political Science Review*, 68, No. 1 (March 1974), 106–112.
10. William J. Keefe and Morris S. Ogul, *The American Legislative Process: Congress and the States*, 3rd ed. (Englewood Cliffs, N.J.: Prentice-Hall, 1973), pp. 124–130.
11. John C. Wahlke et al., *The Legislative System* (New York: John Wiley, 1962), p. 128.
12. James Barber, *The Lawmakers: Recruitment and Adaptation to Legislative Life* (New Haven: Yale University Press, 1965), pp. 19ff.
13. John W. Soule, "Future Political Ambitions and the Behavior of Incumbent State Legislators," *Midwest Journal of Political Science*, 13 (August 1969), 439–454.
14. Alan Rosenthal, *Legislative Performance in the States: Explorations of Committee Behavior* (New York: The Free Press, 1974), chap. 3.
15. Kenneth T. Palmer, "The Pennsylvania General Assembly: Politics and Prospects," in the *Pennsylvania Assembly on State Legislatures in American Politics* (Pittsburgh: University of Pittsburgh Press, 1968), pp. 2–22.
16. Malcolm E. Jewell, *The State Legislature: Politics and Practice* (New York: Random House, 1969), p. 39.
17. Polsby, "The Institutionalization of the U.S. House," p. 164.
18. Kenneth T. Palmer, "The State Legislature" in James F. Horan et al., *Downeast Politics: The Government of the State of Maine* (Dubuque, Ia.: Kendall-Hunt, 1975), chap. 4.
19. Quoted in Jack H. Morris, "A State Legislature is Not Always a Model of Ideal Government," in W. P. Collins, *Perspectives on State and Local Politics* (Englewood Cliffs, N.J.: Prentice-Hall, 1974), p. 82.
20. Yong Hyo Cho and H. George Frederickson, "The Effects of Reapportionment: Subtle, Selective, Limited," *National Civic Review*, 63, No. 7 (July 1974), 357–362.
21. *The Book of the States, 1976–1977* (Lexington, Ky.: The Council of State Governments, 1976).

22. Statistics drawn from relevant editions of *The Book of the States*.
23. Karl A. Bosworth and James W. Fesler, "Legislators and Governors," in James W. Fesler, ed., *The 50 States and their Local Governments* (New York: Knopf, 1967), p. 291.
24. Herbert Kaufman, *Politics and Policies in State and Local Governments* (Englewood Cliffs, N.J.: Prentice-Hall, 1963), pp. 35–44.
25. Ibid.
26. *The Book of the States, 1974–1975* (Lexington, Ky.: The Council of State Governments, 1974)
27. York Wiibern, "Administrative Organization," in Fesler, ed., *The 50 States*, p. 347.
28. Ibid., p. 348.
29. Fred W. Grupp, Jr. and Alan R. Richards, "Variations in Elite Perceptions of American States as Referents for Public Policy Making," *American Political Science Review*, 69, No. 3 (September 1975), pp. 850–858.
30. Deil S. Wright, "Executive Leadership in State Administration," *Midwest Journal of Political Science*, 11, No. 1 (February, 1967), 4.
31. Joseph A. Schlesinger, "The Politics of the Executive," in Herbert Jacob and Kenneth N. Vines, eds., *Politics in the American States*, 2nd ed. (Boston: Little, Brown, 1972), pp. 210–237.
32. Ibid.
33. Cited in Coleman Ransone, *The Office of Governor in the United States* (University, Ala.: University of Alabama Press, 1956), p. 132.
34. Terry Sanford, *Storm Over the States* (New York: McGraw-Hill, 1967), p. 188.
35. William J. Keefe, *The American Legislative Process*, p. 380.
36. See Frank Prescott, "The Executive Veto in the American States," *Western Political Quarterly*, 3, No. 1 (March 1950), 102.
37. Samuel R. Soloman, "Governors: 1960–1970," *National Civic Review*, 60, No. 3 (March 1971), 126–146.
38. Donald P. Sprengel, *Gubernatorial Staffs: Functional and Political Profiles* (Iowa City, Ia.: The University of Iowa—Institute of Public Affairs, 1969), pp. 31–52.
39. See Malcolm E. Jewell, "The Governor as Legislative Leader," in Thad L. Beyle and J. Oliver Williams, *The American Governor in Behavioral Perspective* (New York: Harper and Row, 1972), pp. 127–140.
40. Sarah P. McCally, "The Governor and His Legislative Party," *American Political Science Review*, 60, No. 4 (December 1966), 923–942.
41. Douglas M. Fox, *The Politics of City and State Bureaucracy* (Pacific Palisades, Calif.: Goodyear Publishing Co., 1974), p. 24.
42. Ronald D. Michaelson, "An Analysis of the Chief Executive: How the Governor Uses His Time," *State Government*, 45, No. 3 (Summer 1972), 153–160.
43. *State Government News*, 18, (August 1975), 4.
44. George A. Bell, "State Administrative Organization Activities, 1972–1973," *The Book of the States, 1974–1975* (Lexington, Ky.: The Council of State Governments, 1974), p. 137.
45. *The Book of the States 1976–1977* (Lexington, Ky.: The Council of State Governments, 1976), sect. IV.
46. Daniel R. Grant and H. C. Nixon, *State and Local Government in America*, 3rd ed. (Boston: Allyn and Bacon, 1975), pp. 324–326.
47. Ira Sharkansky, "Agency Requests, Gubernatorial Support, and Budget Success in State Legislatures," *American Political Science Review*, 62, No. 4 (December 1968), 1,220–1,231.
48. Milton D. Green, "The Business of the Trial Courts," in Harry W. Jones, ed., *The Courts, the Public, and the Law Explosion* (Englewood Cliffs, N.J.: Prentice-Hall, 1965), pp. 12ff. My description relies heavily on Green's account.
49. Ibid., p. 13.
50. Kenneth M. Dolbeare, *Trial Courts in Urban Politics* (New York: John Wiley, 1967), p. 3. Emphasis in original.
51. Quoted in Duane Lockard, *The Politics of State and Local Government* (New York: Macmillan, 1969), p. 454.

52. Dolbeare, *Trial Courts*, pp. 73–74.
53. James W. Hurst, *The Growth of American Law* (Boston: Little, Brown, 1950), p. 88.
54. Stuart S. Nagel, "Political Party Affiliation and Judges' Decisions," *American Political Science Review*, 55 (December 1961), 843–850.
55. Ibid., p. 847.
56. Bradley C. Canon and Dean Jaros, "External Variables, Institutional Structure and Dissent on State Supreme Courts," *Polity*, 3 (Winter 1970), 175–200.
57. Ibid., p. 190.
58. Thomas Dye, *Politics in States and Communities* (Englewood Cliffs, N.J.: Prentice-Hall, 1969), p. 175.
59. Bradley C. Canon, "Characteristics and Patterns of State Supreme Court Justices," *State Government*, 45, No. 1 (Winter 1972), 34–41.
60. Stanley B. Botner, "Personal and Career Characteristics of State Government Administrators," *State Government*, 47, No. 1 (Winter 1974), 54–58.
61. Kenneth N. Vines, "Southern Supreme Courts and Race Relations," *Western Political Quarterly*, 18 (March 1965), 5–18.
62. Henry R. Glick, *Supreme Courts in State Politics* (New York: Basic Books, Inc., 1971), pp. 39–41.
63. John T. Wold, "Political Orientations, Social Backgrounds, and Role Perceptions of State Supreme Court Judges," *Western Political Quarterly*, 27, No. 1 (June 1974), 239–248.
64. Neil T. Romans, "The Role of State Supreme Courts in Judicial Policy Making: *Escobedo, Miranda*, and the Use of Judicial Impact Analysis," *Western Political Quarterly*, 27, No. 1 (March 1974), 38–59.
65. Henry R. Glick and Kenneth N. Vines, *State Court Systems* (Englewood Cliffs, N.J.: Prentice-Hall, 1973), pp. 95–96.
66. Winston W. Crouch et. al., *California Government and Politics*, 4th ed. (Englewood Cliffs, N.J.: Prentice-Hall, 1967), p. 219.

Chapter V

POLICY OUTPUTS
IN THE STATES

Within the state political system, the end products resulting from the work of input and decision-making agencies are public policies. These policies, or authoritative decisions of the states, span many areas. They include the maintenance of the decision-making agencies themselves — for instance, the staffing of state agencies and the apportioning of state legislatures. They also embrace various ceremonial activities, such as honoring distinguished state citizens and establishing certain state holidays. But the policies that concern us are those associated with the states' struggle to respond to the major stresses within their environments or, more specifically, to the demands growing from these stresses. To survive as a political system, the states constantly allocate and reallocate their basic resources — money, skills, services — to satisfy popular demands and to settle conflicts among their citizens.

This chapter looks at the basic public programs in the states as revealed by their budgets and then considers the ways in which the states' environments and input and decision-making agencies shape these policies. Although political science has for centuries been interested in the official allocation of rewards, benefits, penalties, and deprivations in society, concern over policy analysis has intensified over the past few years. Numerous scholars now hold that "public policy is

the main dependent variable that political science seeks to explain."[1]
The political system model highlights policy by focusing attention on the
"authoritative decisions" of political systems and on the power relationships that mold such decisions. In the field of U. S. state politics in
particular, there has been a significant outpouring of literature over the
past decade concerned with the general problem of public policies.
Until the early 1960s research in state politics paid relatively scant
attention to the matter of what the states did in terms of monies they
spent and the kinds of regulations they adopted. Investigations of state
politcs tended, instead, to center on the three dimensions of state
political systems discussed in chapters 2, 3, and 4 — political environment, political inputs, and decision-making agencies. Now, however, researchers are striving to use much of this knowledge to explain
policy outcomes in the states, especially variations in programs among
the states.

Raising and Spending Money

To begin an analysis of state programs, let us consider the main
sources of state monies and the principal purposes for which they are
expended. We will use fiscal year 1974 as a focus for our discussion. As
suggested in chapter 1, the states have been a major growth sector in the
American economy in recent years; in the mid-1970s their total spending was nearly double the level at the start of the decade.

In 1974 the general revenues available to the states amounted
to $122,327 million; their total general spending came to $119,891
million.[2] One key source of state funds lay entirely outside the state
political system, or at least state politicians were not required to oversee
its enforcement and collection from their citizens. Federal grants-in-aid
and general revenue sharing supplied about one-fourth of the dollars
($31,632 million) in state treasuries in 1974. The major programs
supported by federal grants were public welfare (45 percent of the total
federal grant-in-aid package), education (23 percent), and highways (15
percent). Over the past five years welfare grants have risen from a third
to nearly half of the federal aids; in contrast, highways declined as a
portion of federal assistance from one quarter of the aid package in 1969
to about one-sixth in 1974. Through the use of matching formulas,
whereby the state typically raises one dollar for each two contributed by
the federal government, federal aids help to encourage state policy
innovation. Grants-in-aid contribute toward maintaining a floor under
people's living standards (as in welfare) and toward accomplishing
national objectives through state participation (as in building the
interstate highway system).

It should be noted, however, that grant-in-aid money is frequently allocated to the states on bases other than state per capita wealth (for example, in highway programs, in which geographical features are important considerations). For this reason, federal grants do not appear to redistribute state resources — that is, they do not mainly transfer dollars from rich to poorer states. Contrary to popular impression, economists have found that "taken as a whole, federal grants-in-aid tend to be concentrated neither in the wealthy nor in the poor states."[3]

State Revenues. Within the states, the largest single producer of funds in 1974 was the general sales tax, used by all but five states. In that year the general sales tax raised 18.5 percent of the states' revenues. General sales taxes in the states are of comparatively recent vintage (Mississippi was the first to employ such a tax in 1932). Given local government's reliance on property taxes and the federal government's dependence on income taxes, however, sales taxes rapidly became the major tool for state governments.[4] At the present time citizens in most states pay at a rate of about 4 percent. The states typically have provisions exempting from the sales tax such necessities as food, medicines, and sometimes clothing. Still, the general sales tax remains a regressive tax, inasmuch as it forces lower income groups to pay a higher proportion of their earnings than wealthier groups must pay.

Selective sales taxes, also commonly used in the states, are more defensible in economic terms. They place the burden on the buyers of luxuries and of specific governmental services. The leading selective sales taxes are those on motor fuels and cigarettes (applicable in all states) and on alcoholic beverages (applicable in all states where distribution is not a state monopoly). In 1974 revenues from selective sales taxes amounted to 14.7 percent of the total monies collected by the states. Grouped together and counted as one item, sales taxes in the states produced one-third (33.2 percent) of state revenues in 1974.

A third major source of revenue for the states in 1974 consisted of taxes on personal and corporate income. Wisconsin instituted a personal income tax in 1911, before the first legal federal income tax, but the states generally did not opt for this levy until the 1930s. As of 1974, forty-four states employed an income tax. In a few instances, it applied only to certain types of residents (in New Jersey, commuters) or to certain kinds of income (in New Hampshire, dividend and interest income only). The median rate of the state personal income tax runs about 20 percent of the federal income tax. In 1974 personal income taxes raised 14 percent of the states' total revenues. In some states, including New York, Oregon, Wisconsin, Massachusetts, and Delaware, the income tax has long been the main revenue source, contributing up to 40 percent of state monies. Also in 1974 forty-six states employed a corporation income tax; this levy produced 4.9 percent of the revenues available to the fifty states in that year. Income taxes combined, then, yielded 18.9 percent of the funds going into state coffers in 1974.

Federal grants-in-aid, sales taxes, and income taxes made up about three-fourths of the revenues collected by the states in 1974. The remaining dollars were raised from a variety of sources, mostly charges and license fees. All states collect a motor vehicle tax through the annual sale of license plates or stickers for old plates. A few states tax vehicles as part of the owner's personal property, but most vary the tax according to the car's weight and horsepower. Such fees provided the states with about $3.5 billion, or 2.8 percent of their income. Tuition and other payments at state-supported institutions of higher education constituted another large item in the "charges and fees" category in 1974. The revenue raised in this way totaled $5.4 billion, or 4.4 percent of states' income. Other sources contributing more than one percent of state monies in 1974 were interest earnings (2.6 percent), death and gift taxes (1.2 percent, hospitals (1.2 percent), and property taxes (1.1 percent). We may note that lotteries, which were widely heralded as a new income source for state governments a few years ago, seem to produce relatively small amounts of revenue. In 1974 proceeds from lotteries in the twelve states using these games amounted to $317 million, or about 1 percent of these states' combined general revenues.

State Expenditures. Now let us look at the other side of the ledger and examine how the states expended their funds in the same year. By all indicators, the largest and most important activity supported by the states is public education. In 1974 the states spent a total of $46.9 billion, or 39.1 percent of their budgets, on maintaining and expanding their educational systems. In the rapid rise of state budgets over the past fifteen years, education has led all other functional fields. In 1959 total expenditures for education consumed only 31.0 percent of the states' budgets.

About two-thirds of the education budget in the states is spent in the form of grants-in-aid to local school districts. The twentieth century has witnessed a gradual centralization of public school standards and practices in the hands of the state government, a trend that has been fueled by state assumption of more and more local school costs. Whereas in 1900 the states provided only 17 percent of the costs of running public schools, by 1964 the states contributed over 40 percent of the total funds spent for primary and secondary schools. The states set the taxing and borrowing limits of local districts and make rules concerning the number of days schools must be in session, the minimum salaries and qualifications of teachers, and the content of curricula.[5] A major task of the states is to equalize educational opportunities in their various localities through the use of subsidy formulas designed to favor poor districts. In recent years the states have pursued this goal in part through the consolidation of local school districts. (Less than one quarter of the districts — many of the "little red school house" variety — that were in existence in the early 1950s were still operating in the 1970s.)

The remaining one-third of the states' education budgets goes to public higher education. The states have long taken pride in their role in providing higher education opportunities. As one scholar has observed: "A key element in the American dream, advancement and success by means of education and technical training, has always been associated with state governments. The state university is the one institution in which all citizens of the state, except those wealthy enough to send their children elsewhere, have a direct or potential interest."[6] Increases in spending in this area in the 1960s were nothing short of dramatic: in response to rapidly expanding student populations, the states increased their expenditure for higher education nearly fourfold between 1959 and 1969 (from $2,614 million to $10,004 million). In the 1970s, on the other hand, public higher education has found itself hard-pressed to maintain its share of the state budget in the face of an austerity economy and a stabilizing of student enrollments. In the five years between 1969 and 1974 total spending for higher education increased almost 60 percent, but the share represented by higher education of overall state budgets declined from 15 percent in 1969 to a little under 13 percent in 1974. In order to establish cost and quality controls over this enterprise, statewide systems of higher education have been adopted in recent years to coordinate the work of all or nearly all publicly supported units.

Public welfare is the second major functional activity of the states, as measured by dollars expended. In 1974 the states spent 18.8 percent of their budgets on welfare programs. This figure represents a modest increase over the past decade (in 1969, the proportion of state budgets going to welfare was 16.0 percent). The basic structure of the present-day welfare system was established in the 1930s, when under the Roosevelt administration the federal government assumed a major responsibility for the nation's public welfare programs; previously welfare administration had rested mainly in the hands of state and local governments and with private institutions and charities. The federal government presently pays about 60 percent of the total welfare costs in the country. But the states participate significantly in most programs; for some activities, states and localities share primary responsibility for management.[7]

State welfare programs can be divided into three broad categories.

In the first group are public assistance programs, or categorical programs, as these are sometimes called, on which the states spend a bit more than half of their welfare monies. These programs, which are supported in part by federal grants-in-aid, offer cash assistance to persons falling into specific categories of need. Since the 1930s they have included aid to the blind, aid to dependent children, and old-age assistance; in 1950 a program of aid to the permanently disabled was created; and in the 1960s most states added programs of medical assistance to this list. For needy persons not belonging to one of these categories, all states maintain programs of general assistance that they finance entirely out of their own funds. A second type of state welfare work is in the field of social insurance. The two leading programs are unemployment compensation and workmen's compensation (for job-related injury or sickness). The states finance and administer these activities on their own, subject only to generalized standards. Finally the states maintain various institutions for people unable to care for themselves even with financial assistance; included here are homes for the elderly and the ill and state orphanages. Most states work closely with their local governments in administering welfare assistance. In 1974 about one-third of the states' welfare budgets went to local governments in the form of intergovernmental payments.

The third largest activity financed by the states is the maintenance and construction of highways. In 1974 highways consumed 13.2 percent of state budgets across the country. Although the proportion of state spending represented by highways has declined steadily in recent years (in 1969 it was 18.4 percent), highways are an activity of formidable political significance in many states.[8] In the twentieth century the states were the key level of government in the federal system responsible for providing modern road networks. Beginning around 1920 "good roads associations," consisting of auto users, truckers, oil and gas producers, contractors, and other organizations, won victory after victory in state politics in their pursuit of surfaced streets and highways. The special importance of roads in rural areas undoubtedly aided the cause of these highway lobbies in the state capital, to which rural groups already had considerable access.

The upshot of these pressures was to center highway spending and decisions concerning classification, location, construction, rights-of-way, and weight limits in the hands of a state highway department or state highway commission. In most states the highway department has long been independent or partially independent of the governor. About half of the states prohibit diversion of highway funds (such as funds collected from gas taxes) for purposes other than that of road maintenance and construction. Most highway money is expended directly by the state; the states in 1974 turned over to their local governments only about one-fifth of their highway revenues. During the 1970s, however, a revision of priorities in the transportation field is ending the traditional power and independence of state highway departments. The most critical current problems are associated with the shortage of mass transit facilities in metropolitan areas. A number of states have responded to this problem by transforming their state departments of highways into state departments of transportation. Under the new administrative arrangements, commuter transit facilities are placed more or less on a par with rural-based highway lobbies in competition for state funds. As urban groups become more active in state politics, highway departments will likely lose much of the independence they have long enjoyed and devote more attention to the transportation needs of large cities and their suburbs.

Education, welfare, and highways together consumed a total of 71.1 percent of the expenditures made by the states in 1974. Other activities supported by the states that took over two percent of their total expenditures in that year were health and hospitals (7.1 percent), general local government support (4.0 percent), natural resources (2.5 percent), interest on state debt (2.4 percent), and corrections and police (2.6 percent). It is useful to recall that these statistics are averages drawn from fifty state budgets looked at collectively. Although education, welfare, and highways are leading activities in every state, the actual proportions of individual state budgets that they represent vary. Such differences become even more marked when we consider the smaller specialized programs that individual states offer to their citizens.

As an example of the variations that exist in state spending patterns, we may consider the budgets of California and New York for 1974. In that year the two states spent comparable total dollar amounts (California: $13,702 million; New York: $14,116 million). These figures conceal important differences in individual functional areas. California expended almost twice as much for public higher education than did New York ($1,438 million as against $807 million), and slightly exceeded the Empire State in subsidies to localities for primary and secondary education ($3,455 million as against $3,167 million). On the other hand, New York devoted more funds ($234 million) to tuition grants, fellowships, and aid to private schools than did California ($99 million). California outspent New York in the area of highways ($1,177 million as against $828 million), but New York spent far more on housing and urban renewal ($385 million compared to $3 million). California spent slightly more money for public welfare ($3,556 million) than did New York ($3,331 million), but in the related field of health and hospitals New York ($1,356 million) led California ($605 million). Finally, California far exceeded the Empire State in spending on natural resources ($428 million as against $147 million), but in the special category of airports New York ($29 million) was well ahead of California ($2 million). Each state's budgeting reflects distinctive policy choices designed to accommodate the pressures and demands of that state's economic arrangements and political processes. It is in these choices that the states frequently differ widely and importantly.

What Determines Policy Differences?

The variations in expenditures between New York and California lead us to consider what has become a major intellectual goal in the study of state politics. Over the past several years scholars have devoted increasing attention to identifying and understanding the factors that account for policy variations in the states. Investigators have sought to understand the relationships between particular characteristics of state political systems (such as political party alignments or legislative behavior) and state public policies. The goal has been to establish which elements seem most important in creating differences in state public programs.

Obviously part of the importance of this work is intellectual: determining links among the states' environments, inputs, decision-making agencies, and the public policies and services that they provide their citizens contributes not only to our understanding of the U. S. states but also of other types of political systems. But there is also a more practical reason for this research. If as citizens we wish our state to undertake new programs, or to increase expenditures in certain areas, we must identify the factors most closely related to the states' willingness (or refusal) to deal with such issues. For instance, to what extent does reapportionment lead a state to a more intensive concern with the problems of metropolitan areas? Will the rise of a two-party system lead to more generous treatment by a state of the problems of the poor? What is the relative significance of certain "given" factors — such as urbanism and per capita income — compared with elements more directly subject to human molding — such as the structure of the state legislature — in accounting for policy differences? These are serious practical questions to ask about the states in the 1970s, in addition to being matters of theoretical interest.

Early Assumptions and Initial Findings

We can best begin consideration of the determinants of state policy outputs by briefly examining the development of research in state politics. To the extent that the writing on U. S. state politics in the 1950s and early 1960s is subject to classification, a reasonable assessment is that it generally emphasized what we have called the "inputs" of state politics. Studies of individual states during this period seemed to take their lead from the landmark explorations of political party patterns in the South and in the nation by V. O. Key, Jr.[9] In a survey of thirteen monographs published in these years (covering individual states), one investigator has determined that very nearly half of their content was devoted to three closely related topics: political parties, elections, and voting behavior.[10] This is not to say that political scientists in the 1950s were uninterested in other dimensions of state politics. The focus on parties and elections merely suggests that students of state politics — like those in most other academic fields — have acquired their know-ledge unevenly. Investigators had not yet fashioned the conceptual tools necessary to undertake detailed examination of state political environments and state public policies, topics of greater interest today.

If they were not able to pursue a systematic study of the nature and causes of public policies in the states, political scientists nonetheless made certain assumptions in the 1950s about the impact on public policy of the political elements that they did study. For the most part, students assumed that characteristics of the political system were important in shaping different policy outcomes. Variations in such features would, they thought, lead to changes in the programs on which the state spent (or failed to spend) money. Possibly the most insightful discussion of the relationship between party systems and public policies (recalling that political parties were the central topic of study during this period) was Key's analysis of the policy consequences of the factional systems he found in the southern states. Key believed that the disorganized factional arrangement (the "multifactional" systems in particular) in the South tended to result in very conservative public policies — that is, policies favorable to the interests of the socially privileged. He wrote:

> The significant question is, who benefits from political dis-organization? Its significance is equalled only by the difficulty of arriving at an answer. There probably are several answers, de-pending on the peculiar circumstances in each case. Politics generally comes down, over the long run, to a conflict between those who have and those who have less. In state politics the crucial issues tend to turn around taxation and expenditure. . . . It follows that the grand objective of the haves is obstruction, at least of the haves who take only a short-term view. Organization is not always necessary to obstruct; it is essential, however, for the promotion of a sustained program in behalf of the have-nots, although not all

party or factional organization is dedicated to that purpose. It follows, if these propositions are correct, that over the long-run the have-nots lose in a disorganized politics. They have no mechanism through which to act and their wishes find expression in fitful rebellions led by transient demagogues who gain their confidence but often have neither the technical competence nor the necessary stable base of political power to effectuate a program.[11]

Key's comment, if expanded to cover the fifty states, could lead to the following hypothesis: states having one-party systems may be expected to be less generous in their public expenditures for have-not groups than states with two-party systems. In two-party states, low-income voters enjoy a political choice at the polls that they do not really possess in one-party states. They thus presumably can force the parties (in a two-party state) to be more responsive to their needs. This example has focused on parties, but much the same reasoning was applied to the relationship between legislative apportionment and public policy in the 1950s. Observers typically attributed the foot-dragging tendencies of the states in that period to malapportioned state legislatures. Once the state assemblies were fairly apportioned, they speculated, the states would be more willing to deal with the problems of an urban society.

By the mid-1960s, the growth of interest in state political processes led researchers to test in detail these kinds of assumptions linking politics to policies. Their guiding question was: What factors account for differences among the states in the kinds of public policies they enact? Although the question was not new, the research strategies used to seek answers at this point reflected the rise of quantitative methods in the study of political science. Most studies involved the determining of the correlations that existed between two or more variables in state politics. For example, suppose we want to know whether the traditional under-representation of urban areas in state legislatures really led the states to underfinance their cities — as measured by state expenditures to local governments — in favor of rural areas. To find an answer (and to oversimplify the procedure somewhat) we would draw up two lists. One list would rank the fifty states according to the degree to which they discriminated against their cities in the allocation of legislative seats (let us say, as of the year 1961, just before the handing down of *Baker* v. *Carr*). The states would be listed from one (the worst apportioned state) to fifty (the most equitably apportioned state.) In our second list, we would rank the states according to the degree to which they discriminated against their cities in terms of financial aid (again, as of the year 1961). The states would be listed from one (the state in which city dwellers received the least state funds per capita as compared to rural residents) to fifty (the state in which city residents received the most state funds per capita as compared to rural citizens). The next, and most crucial, step is to determine the extent to which the rankings of the states on the two lists are similar. If some reformers' assumptions about the consequences of malapportionment are correct, the worst apportioned states should also be states providing the least monies for their urban residents (high correlation). On the other hand, if the lists show little resemblance (low correlation) to each other, we may conclude that legislative apportionment itself has little to do with state expenditures for urban areas.

Beginning about 1963 numerous studies of this type were undertaken. Investigators examined the relationships among several political system characteristics (including voter turnout and political party competition) and a variety of measures of public policy. These measures included such welfare variables as old-age assistance payments, average payment per recipient of aid to the blind, and average payments per family for aid to dependent children; such highway variables as the distribution of state highway funds to municipal highway extensions; and such education variables as the average per-pupil expenditure in the states.[12] The goal was to determine the relative importance of the various factors that seemed to shape policy outcomes in the states.

The Significance of Economic Differences. The results of these initial studies were often surprising and depressing. On the whole, the research yielded little support for the idea that variations in the political features of the states led to significant differences in their public programs. Instead, investigations showed that such economic variables as per capita income, urbanism, and industrialization, accounted for most of the differences that had previously been attributed to political matters. Those states that most generously supported various public programs and services were mainly states with high levels of economic development. To be sure, researchers did find that two-party states usually spent more for public services than did one-party states. But further testing indicated that the relationship was largely spurious: two-party states spent more not because they had two-party competition but because they had higher levels of wealth and industrialization than one-party states enjoyed. When wealth was statistically controlled, the link between party competition and public spending almost disappeared. In *Politics, Economics, and the Public*, probably the most widely discussed book on state politics in the mid-1960s, Thomas Dye concluded:

> Differences in the policy choices of states with different types
> of political systems turn out to be largely a product of differing

socioeconomic levels rather than a direct product of political variables. Levels of urbanization, industrialization, income, and education appear to be more influential in shaping policy outcomes than political system characteristics.[13]

Apart from its having statistical support, the Dye argument seems to conform with what we know theoretically about the operation of the state political system. In the two preceding chapters, we noted that state input and decision-making agencies traditionally have been loosely organized and rather undifferentiated from their state environments. The Dye thesis appears to carry this point one step further by saying that political agencies have indeed been so poorly organized that they have not been able to make their own mark on state public policies. Instead, the link apparently has been almost a direct one between the environment of a state and its public programs, with but a minor role played by intervening agencies — parties, legislative bodies, and the like.

The "economic determinism" argument is important and challenging, but it also has limitations.[14] One criticism is that in a field as complex as politics, no single variable or set of variables can be expected to "explain" a high proportion of variation within a set of dependent variables. To illustrate, one scholar has calculated that the four economic variables that Thomas Dye employed in *Politics, Economics, and the Public* (education, industrialization, urbanism, and per capita wealth) explained on an average only 36.75 percent of the variation in the fifty-four policy variables Dye examined for the fifty states.[15] This was a higher percentage than Dye's four political variables were able to explain (he used voter turnout, party competition, percentage of Democratic control of the state government, and degree of malapportionment), but it still leaves much of the difference associated with policy outcomes to be accounted for by other, as yet unexplored, factors. We cannot be sure of the relative significance of economic and political variables until we examine many additional factors — for instance, political attitudes, interest group strength, the performance of executive and legislative institutions, and so forth.

A second general objection leveled against the initial policy studies is that much as they limited themselves to a very few input variables, so they focused on a severely restricted number of public policy measures. Investigators relied almost entirely on dollars spent for this or for that program as evidence of policy differences among states. Dollar figures are a useful measure, but sole reliance on them as symbols of what the states do in their many areas of service to their electorates is likely to lead to distortions. All states are involved in programs that cannot be measured adequately by dollars expended. For instance, the states vary in their regulatory policies toward private enterprise and public utilities; they vary in certain sumptuary laws, especially those dealing with alcoholic beverages; and they vary in numerous social programs, such as prison administration and the rehabilitation of drug addicts. These activities — for which budgeted dollar amounts may provide but a remote idea of state performance — need more examination (and the development of accurate indicators of performance) before we can establish how important political factors are in determining what states do.

Current Findings: The Mix of Politics and Economics

In the past decade critics of the initial policy studies have produced a literature of their own stressing that politics *do* count in several significant areas of state policy making. The scholarly issue at the present time is not whether politics *or* economics is most critical in determining what states do, but what weight each has in shaping particular state functions and programs. A combination of political and economic factors is involved in most areas of state policy. The discussion here outlines recent findings, noting especially the political system variables that have been shown to affect state outputs.

Political Dimensions of State Environments. One body of research has focused on state environmental differences. Recent investigations have identified a number of political variables associated with the environments of states that are significant in shaping policy differences. These political factors are important in that they add to earlier studies that focused almost exclusively on such economic determinants as per capita income. One key political variable is the idea of political culture noted in chapter 2. The categorization of states into moralistic, individualistic, and traditionalistic groups (under the Elazar formulation) helps to predict levels of political participation and public spending. Under similar economic conditions, moralistic states tend to have greater voter turnouts in elections and to provide a more generous set of public services for their citizens than states with other political cultures.

A second environmental factor is that of social and cultural diversity. States in which citizens differ widely in income, education, ethnic background, religion, and occupation tend to have more open political systems, to offer more programs aimed at less fortunate members of society, and to have less discrimination than those states where citizens constitute a more homogeneous population.[16] The underlying reason for this is as follows: In a state with a diverse population, different groups of people — each with its own program — find it necessary to work together to form a political majority. In so doing, most groups will get at least some of their demands met. The importance of diversity as a key element in the states' political environments is further supported by investigation of the interesting variable of religious fundamentalism. One analysis shows that the higher the percentage of people in a state adhering to a religious denomination believing in a literal interpretation of the Bible, the lower the level of the state's political participation, party competition, and willingness to spend for public services.[17] This particular cultural variable turned out to be a more accurate predictor of differences in expenditures for public services in the states than did variations in per capita income.

The Impact of State Decision-making Agencies. Scholars have also paid more attention to decision-making agencies in exploring the determinants of public policy in the states. Part of the reason that early studies found few links between input agencies (such as political parties) and policy outputs in the states is that these investigations overlooked the mediating influence of legislative and executive bodies. Political parties are effective in making policy only when they can turn party conflict into public policy, and this work is done in elected political agencies. Edward Carmines has found that the relationship between party competition and welfare expenditures is quite close in those states having professionalized (or institutionalized) legislatures.[18] The higher the degree of party competition, the higher the expenditure per capita the states made for welfare programs where the states had well-paid, well-staffed legislative bodies. On the other hand, in states with relatively "amateurish" legislatures, the relationship between party competition and welfare spending largely disappears. Carmines's analysis provides a basis for believing that improvements in legislative operations can make a difference in translating demands for programs into relevant public policy.

Political and Economic Factors Affecting State Budgets. With regard to state budgets generally (that is, the total dollars raised and expended by the individual states) the relative importance of economic and political factors as determinants depends on how we frame our problem. If we are interested in state-local budgets of all the states taken together, the main determinants seem related to economics. As early as 1952 one economist found in a study of combined operating expenditures of state and local governments that three variables — per capita income, population density, and percentage of persons living in urban places — explained 72 percent of the interstate variation.[19] Of the factors examined, per capita income was by far the most important. In his *Politics, Economics, and the Public,* Dye also considered state-local spending, and his work generally confirmed earlier findings. He found, for instance, that per capita income itself accounted for about two-thirds of the differences among the states in the tax dollars that they and their local governments collected. As people's income rises, so does the capacity of state and local governments to secure greater tax yields.

Every state strikes its own balance of revenue raising between the state government and local governments. In rural states in the South and Great Plains, the state government tends to raise the bulk of the total state-local tax monies collected. In the larger, more industrialized states, state governments depend heavily on their local governments to raise their own funds. Studies looking only at state spending have found that per capita income — and economic factors generally — are very weakly related to interstate differences.[20] Instead, the variables most closely associated with differences in state spending are more political in nature. Two of the most interesting political factors may be called *incrementalism* and *elite behavior*.

Incrementalism refers to the idea that governmental budget makers tend to rely heavily on past expenditure levels in deciding on present-day spending. When an incrementalist approach is taken, administrators and legislators do not attempt to review comprehensively the goals for which monies are being sought. Whole programs are not reviewed from scratch and priorities among programs are not newly established in order to assign the available resources. In a study of budgeting in Illinois, one observer noted:

> Decision-makers make choices in situations which typically present limited alternatives among policies that are only incrementally different from existing policies — i.e. the choice normally is not between this new program or that new program, but between additions to or subtractions from ongoing programs.[21]

Although found at all governmental levels, incrementalism seems especially embedded at the state level, mainly because of traditional weaknesses in state institutions. State budgeters rarely have the staff, time, and data to do much more than make marginal adjustments in existing programs. The incremental nature of changes in state budgets is seen in the fact that high-spending states and low-spending states continue to hold their place over many decades. Ira Sharkansky has found a significant correlation between the ranking of the states in dollars spent per capita in 1903 and their ranking in dollars spent in 1965. Budgets had increased more than a hundredfold during this period, but the highest- and lowest-spending states in 1903 continued to be the largest and smallest spenders in 1965.[22]

In a sense, of course, a focus on the variable of incrementalism begs a more fundamental question: How did states arrive at their particular level of spending in the first place? An answer to this leads us to examine state histories, or what Richard Hofferbert calls "politically relevant incidents" in states, in which the work of an activist governor, or some other set of events, caused the state to alter its traditional ways of doing things.[23] Incrementalism does not preclude a state from occasionally breaking away from its past and establishing new levels of spending and services. The political incidents associated with changes in spending levels usually center around the variable of elite behavior. The actions of human beings are, of course, a vital consideration in all policy analysis; despite the seeming determinism in the relationships between economic factors and public policy, people have to act before a policy can exist. The impact of political elites seems to be especially pronounced in the area of state budget change.

A good example of a state that recently altered its spending levels is Kentucky.[24] Until the late 1950s Kentucky had generally fitted the incrementalist model of state budgeting; that is, it had only marginally increased its appropriations year by year. Between 1957 and 1962, however, the Blue Grass State increased its rate of spending faster than any other state: its per capita expenditure jumped from $94.60 in 1957 to $209.25 in 1962. The abrupt change was due mainly to two political factors. One was the election of Governor Bert Combs, a politician from the low-income area of eastern Kentucky and the first governor elected from that part of the state in many years. Unlike several of his predecessors, Governor Combs favored increased taxation and spending as a means of fostering the state's economic growth and meeting its social welfare needs.

The second factor was the promotion by the Kentucky legislature of a bill to distribute a veteran's bonus. The bonus measure provided for a small and temporary sales tax to help retire the bonds to be issued for the bonus. The veteran's bonus idea apparently started without the governor's knowledge, and legislators appeared to hope that the governor would veto the bill as being "fiscally irresponsible" (although they felt compelled to vote for it themselves for political reasons). However, Governor Combs instead used the bonus bill as a cover to institute a new, permanent 3 percent sales tax. Faced with the bonus measure and a tax bill tied together as a single package, Kentucky legislators reluctantly supported the proposal. As a result, new revenues were generated that permitted the states's expenditures to move rapidly upward, especially in the fields of education and highways. Each major rise was heralded as a boon to economic development, and Kentucky thus reached a new and politically acceptable level in state governmental spending.

Under what conditions are state spending patterns in general likely to change? Analyses of other states suggest that a state which is experiencing substantial variation in voter turnout and in levels of party competition from one election to the next is most apt to deviate from incremental budgeting. Because of uncertainty about the nature of their electoral coalitions, politicians in these states are inclined to highlight dramatic issues and new directions in state policy in their campaigns.[25]

To review briefly: studies of state budgeting, meaning the total revenues and expenditures of the states, have tentatively concluded that both economic and political determinants are involved. Per capita wealth in particular seems to be a major explanatory variable when state and local expenditures are taken together. On the other hand, analysis of state spending alone has indicated that because of the particular division of state and local responsibilities within each state, economic factors are not good indicators of interstate differences. Instead, state political histories and the activities of state politicians must be considered. Research in this area is incomplete, but there is a basis now for rejecting ideas of economic determinism that seemed to grow out of the policy studies of the mid-1960s.

Political and Economic Factors Affecting Other State Policies. Recent studies also indicate that the mixture of economic and political variables discussed in terms of total state budgets seems also to apply to separate policy areas. In the case of education and welfare, the main economic variable associated with interstate variations appears to be per capita wealth, and the principal political variables seem to relate to voter turnout and party competition.[26] Overall educational spending is mainly a function of a state's per capita income, but educational innovations (where these are not costly) are determined mostly by political variables. Two-party states in which the Democratic party controls the governorship seem to be particularly innovative in education.[27] Partly because welfare occupies a smaller share of the state's budget than does education, spending patterns in this area are more subject to political influences. We have noticed that states with a high degree of two-party competition are likely to have high welfare expenditures if they possess state legislatures that can translate party aspirations into policy. Additionally, one report shows that it makes a difference whether, in the two-party state, one party is able to fully manage the state government for a particular period. States chronically plagued by party control divided between legislative and executive tend to spend less for welfare (holding economic factors constant) than states in which the two popularly chosen branches fall to the same party in a given election.[28]

Interestingly, state programs for highways and for the use and conservation of natural resources are little influenced by the variables most powerfully affecting state activity in education and welfare. Spending for highways and natural resources is mostly a product of the absence of urbanization and industrialization. States having the fewest people living in Standard Metropolitan Statistical Areas and the largest numbers of persons engaged in agriculture-related employment generally are the ones in which road building and conservation programs consume the largest proportion of the state budget. One study has indicated a very slight relationship between party control of state government (Republican states appear to spend a bit more for highways than Democratic states) and spending on such projects, but otherwise political factors do not help in explaining differences in these policy areas.[29] The reason is probably related to the fact that education and welfare issues often generate intense combat between political parties in the states, whereas decisions concerning highways and natural resources rarely polarize major groups in state politics. Decisions over roads especially may involve bargaining among a relatively small number of politicians.

In addition to looking at the levels of expenditures in the states in various functional areas, recent studies have examined the distribution of state funds among different groups of citizens. One investigation examined the allocation of the burdens of revenues and benefits of expenditures across different income classes in the states.[30] For each state, the researchers calculated first how much a state exacted in revenues from the three lowest income classes, and second, how much it spent in the form of aids and services for these groups. A redistribution ratio was thus determined for each state. Some states expended more than three times more money to lower income groups than they collected from them in taxes; for other states, the ratio of redistribution was much less generous. The investigation found that certain political variables — especially political participation, the degree of extension of civil service coverage of state employees, and legislative professionalism — explained more of the variation among the states in redistribution policy than did the traditional economic variables of per capita income and urbanization. A state willing to redistribute its resources from wealthy to needy citizens seems characterized by an attentive and active electorate and state decision-making bodies that are sufficiently professionalized that they can translate political inputs and demands into specific programs of assistance.

So far we have looked briefly at those types of public policy that can be measured by dollars expended. As we noted earlier, all states are involved in programs for which dollar figures are not very helpful as indicators of levels of activity and involvement. Consideration of these programs and assessment of the factors governing their operation are now major concerns of state politics research. A very fruitful study conducted in this area looked at the willingness of different states over time to innovate programs.[31] In this study Jack Walker constructed an innovation index based on an analysis of eighty-eight separate programs that were adopted by at least twenty state legislatures between 1870 and 1965. Programs ranged from very early ones of compulsory school attendance and state highway patrols to recent ones of state planning agencies and state councils of the arts. Each state received a score according to its speed of adopting these programs over the ninety-five – year period. On the innovation scale, New York and Massachusetts ranked highest, and Nevada, Wyoming, and Mississippi, lowest.

Several socioeconomic variables, including urbanism, industrialization, and per capita income, were associated with differences in innovation among the states. The economically highly developed states were generally most likely to adopt new programs. At the same time one political variable — the legislative apportionment systems in the states — was closely related to innovation. For the period from 1930 to 1965, in particular, there was a high positive correlation between the rankings of the states on the innovation scale and the rankings of the states according to a leading index of legislative malapportionment (a measure that especially emphasizes the degree of urban underrepresentation in state legislatures). Importantly, the relationship between apportionment and innovation held up after Walker controlled for socioeconomic factors. Apportionment thus appears to have an independent effect on the states' willingness to work with new ideas. As the author put it, "states which grant their urban areas full representation in the legislature seem to adopt new ideas more rapidly, on the average, than states which discriminate against their cities."[32]

The findings of the Walker study are not inconsistent with earlier research. As we noted, the first policy studies generally used only the indicator of dollars expended in different areas of state policy making. When dollar figures were used, fairly apportioned states did not seem to act much differently from inequitably apportioned states. But the employment of a separate measure of public policy — the willingness of states to innovate — suggests that the apportionment system does make a difference. Other attempts to measure public policy in nonfiscal terms similarly have pointed to the importance of certain political factors in shaping policy outcome differences among the states. For instance, political party control seems to have been a crucial factor in the passage of civil rights legislation in the states during the post – World War II years. A survey of civil rights provisions in states outside the South for the years from 1945 to 1964 noted that passage of this legislation was

three times more frequent when Democrats controlled the state legislature than it was under either Republican or split control.[33] In these
northern states the Democratic party was usually the more liberal of the
two parties with regard to questions of civil rights, and its program
commitments became public policy when it had majorities in both
branches.

Recent policy studies appear to have established that political
factors are important in shaping certain state programs. In this regard,
they have justified the earlier emphasis (in the 1950s) on political system
characteristics as major determinants of differences in the states. At the
same time we have noted the significance of economic constraints. Both
economic and political elements are responsible for differences in state
programs, but the specific determinants tend to vary with individual
policy areas. Continued investigation is necessary to understand more
precisely the variables associated with each area. Highest, perhaps, on
the agenda for state politics research is the development of new creative
measures for activities falling under all four dimensions of the state
political system.

The discussion in this section has focused on the somewhat
technical problem of how much influence certain political and economic
variables have on state public policies. Although this is a matter of
scholarly interest, it is also a question of broad significance for voters and
residents of the several states. When we say that politics counts in
determining interstate differences in certain programs, we are saying
that the people of the states are using political means — input and
decision-making agencies — to accomplish goals that they have set for
themselves. When we find economic factors accounting for interstate
variations, on the other hand, we are really maintaining that the areas
where these factors dominate are ones where program levels are more
or less determined in advance, established by basic environmental
conditions over which people may have little control. If the fifty states
are to flourish as viable social instruments, it seems clear that politics
must count. The record has positive signs in that direction. Historically
wide variations among the several states in the per capita income of their
populations are gradually narrowing. In 1900 the per capita income of
Alabama citizens was less than a quarter (.24) of the per capita income of
California residents, but in 1972 per capita income in Alabama was
about two-thirds (.69) the income level in California. In the light of
similar economic environments, economic variables may become less
important and political factors more significant in shaping public
policies. Entry into state politics by broader coalitions of citizens and the
professionalization of state institutions are, of course, major developments in making politics count. The states today seem better equipped

to establish preferences in policy in accordance with the desires of their citizens than in past decades.

The States in the Intergovernmental System

For analytic purposes, this book has treated the U. S. states as more or less independent political systems. The political relationships we have talked about have been mostly internal ones, namely, the links between the environment, input agencies, decision-making organs, and policy outputs within individual states. Our argument has been that the systems approach provides insight into the problems states face and offers explanations of why the states act as they do. But we need also to reflect on the states from a broader intergovernmental perspective. Increasingly the activities of the fifty states are affected by the relationships they maintain with their national and local partners. We look, therefore, in these concluding comments to the policy role of the states in the total federal structure.

State Centralization. Two present-day developments are especially worthy of attention. One is the gradual centralization of state government in relation to local governments. Discussions of federalism typically notice the growth of national power vis-à-vis subnational units — a trend which has been occurring over several decades — but an equally important centralization has been taking place at the state level. The states are assuming responsibility for functions once assigned principally to localities or shared with localities, and therefore are playing a larger role in the delivery of services within their jurisdictions. At the turn of the century local governments dwarfed the states financially; localities at that time accounted for approximately seven times more U. S. domestic expenditures than did the states. State centralization of financial responsibilities for various public services began in the 1930s, leveled off somewhat in the 1940s and 1950s, and started to rise again in the 1960s.

The current pattern can be understood by comparing the level of responsibility the states and their localities had for certain functional areas (such as highways, health, education, natural resources, and housing) for the years 1957 and 1969.[34] In 1957 nine states had what might be called centralized services, meaning that the states in this category contributed an average of 55 percent or more of the funds and personnel across a total of fifteen functional areas. By 1969 the number of state governments with this degree of involvement in public services had increased to fifteen states. In a similar vein, the number of states that once relied heavily on their localities for the carrying out of policies and programs has sharply declined. In 1957 some thirteen states contributed less than 40 percent of the personnel and funds involved in fifteen key functional areas. By 1969 that figure had decreased to five states. The decade of the 1960s, which witnessed major initiatives by the national government in domestic policy, also found the states gaining new authority in relation to local governments.

What are the causes of state centralization? One factor is the greater strength of state tax systems. Historically, property taxes accounted for the overwhelming proportion of revenues raised at both the state and local levels. As late as 1913, for instance, property taxes accounted for nearly half (46 percent) of the monies raised by state governments. In subsequent years individual income and sales taxes began to take the place of property taxes as state revenue sources; by the early 1950s these levies comprised over 50 percent of state tax collections. Localities, of course, have continued to rely on property taxes for the bulk of their revenues. Income and sales taxes have proved less regressive than property taxes and, additionally, more elastic or responsive to economic changes. Another cause of state centralization is the need for interlocal cooperation. Such problems as environmental protection and mass transit cannot be addressed except by the concerted action of many communities. In these policy areas the states must frequently guide the cooperative efforts of localities. Colorado, Vermont, and Florida have established comprehensive land-use programs to which local authorities must, in differing degrees, conform.[35] In Maryland, the state has assumed responsibility for public transportation in the Baltimore metropolitan area. The years ahead are likely to find a continuing erosion of local autonomy as community policy problems are pushed upward to the state government.

State Participation in National Programs. A second — and related — development affecting the place of the states in the federal system is their increasing involvement in the formulation and administration of national domestic programs. The states play a key role in experimenting with new policies, but the primary policy-setting agency for the nation is, of course, the federal government. Because in our society public problems in one state or area affect other states or areas, national action of some form is usually required in dealing with most of our social and economic ills. We may recall from chapter 2 that once Congress establishes a policy, the states are bound under constitutional law (as interpreted by the U. S. Supreme Court) to subordinate their own programs to the national standard. The emphasis in this volume on improvements in the states does not detract from the proposition that the federal government designs the fundamental outlines of the federal structure.

But the federal government now depends on the work of the states in achieving its domestic goals. With the declining role of localities as policy setters, the national government has come to rely on the states for help in managing national programs within their domains. Through various devices the federal government has encouraged state governments to coordinate the uses of federal aid monies in their jurisdictions. One technique is the so-called A-95 review power, which was established by the Office of Management and Budget (part of the Executive Office of the president) in 1969.[36] The A-95 review power as it applies to state governments requests that a state planning department (or similar staff agency) comment on applications for federal funds that a state department administering a specific policy area may make. The purpose of the A-95 review power is to insure that when a state applies for a federal aid program· let us say one involving economic development, the proposal will be of concern not only to the economic development department in the state government, but also to state agencies involved in such areas as environmental protection, conservation, land use, and social service delivery systems.

Federal programs directed at cities also employ a state review power. Under the Community Development Act of 1974, cities applying to the U. S. Department of Housing and Urban Development for funds must submit their applications to a state planning agency for comment on the environmental impact of their proposals. In addition, the federal government has encouraged the states to establish their own substate districts for planning purposes and for the coordination of federal and state programs. Forty states had set up such districts as of 1972.[37] Substate districts are usually delineated in a manner much more appropriate to contemporary needs than are traditional county boundaries.

Apart from enlisting the states in the implementation of national programs, the federal government has assisted the states directly in their efforts to strengthen their management capabilities. Under the Intergovernmental Personnel Act (IPA) of 1970, for instance, the national government provides grants to the states for personnel improvement. The act established an IPA Mobility Program under which state personnel may take temporary assignment in federal agencies to gain technical expertise in various policy areas.[38] We should note that state budgets reflect a growing interest in management needs. From 1972 to 1974 state spending for "general control" functions, which refers to money for staffing state decision-making agencies — the governor's office, legislatures, and courts, principally — increased about 50 percent faster than did expenditures for programs. The states are no longer mainly conduits through which federal dollars flow into local treasuries; they are becoming significant mechanisms for control and policy direction in the federal system.

Conclusion

This chapter has considered public policies in the states, with particular reference to how and why states differ in their policies. Both economic and political characteristics of the states appear important in shaping the programs they develop for their citizens. In addition, the states are assuming critical new responsibilities within American federalism. The states' intergovernmental role is related in an important way to internal changes in the states — especially the modernization and democratization of state politics — which earlier chapters have fully discussed. This relationship speaks to the states' emerging place in the American polity.

As political systems the individual states not only share in decisions with national and local governmental units; they also respond in a fundamental way to the needs of their separate populations. In his defense of the assignment of greater powers to the federal government in 1787, James Madison observed that under the new Constitution the states would be watchdogs: they would act — according to Madison — "to detect or to defeat a conspiracy" by the central government "against the liberty of their common constituents."[39] The conspiracies against which the states must guard today may be more technological than political. The technical complexity of government makes it very difficult for average citizens to understand public policy, even programs that directly affect them.[40] This is true for both the federal and state governments, but the states have the crucial advantage of being closer to their citizens. The states can educate people concerning the operation of federal programs, and can try to adjust these programs to meet the needs of their citizens. National associations of governors, state legislators, and other state officials are becoming vital links between state electorates and policy-making agencies in Washington.

The states thus have a dual task: to develop policies for their citizens in the many areas where the federal government has not spoken, and to help shape and monitor domestic programs where the national government has acted. For nearly two centuries a source of weakness, the states' middle position is presently one of unparalleled opportunity to further our national democracy.

NOTES

1. Richard E. Dawson and James A. Robinson, "Inter-Party Competition, Economic Variables, and Welfare Policies in the American States," *Journal of Politics*, 25 (May 1963), 266.
2. Unless otherwise noted, data from this section have been drawn from the following sources: *State Government Finances in 1974* (Washington, D.C.: U.S. Department of Commerce, Bureau of the Census, 1975); *State Government Finances in 1969* (Washington, D.C.: U.S. Department of Commerce, Bureau of the Census, 1970); *Summary of State Finances in 1959* (Washington, D.C.: U.S. Department of Commerce, Bureau of the Census, 1960); *Federal-State-Local Finances: Significant Features of Fiscal Federalism, 1973-74 Edition* (Washington, D.C.: Advisory Commission on Intergovernmental Relations, 1974). I discuss general fund moneys only.
3. George F. Break, *Intergovernmental Fiscal Relations in the United States* (Washington, D.C.: The Brookings Institution, 1967), p. 120.
4. For a more detailed discussion, see Clara Penniman, "The Politics of Taxation," in Herbert Jacob and Kenneth N. Vines, eds., *Politics in the American States*, 3rd ed. (Boston: Little, Brown, 1976), pp. 428–465.
5. See Frederick M. Wirt, "Education Politics and Policies," in Jacob and Vines, eds., *Politics*, 2nd ed. (1971) pp. 284–347.
6. York Wilbern, "States as Components in an Areal Division of Powers," in Arthur Maass, ed., *Area and Power* (Glencoe, Ill.: The Free Press, 1959), pp. 87–88.
7. See Robert Albritton, "Welfare Policy," in Jacob and Vines, eds., *Politics*, pp. 349–387.
8. See Robert S. Friedman, "State Politics and Highways," in Jacob and Vines, eds., *Politics*, pp. 477–519.
9. V. O. Key, Jr., *Southern Politics in State and Nation* (New York: Knopf, 1949) and *American State Politics: An Introduction* (New York: Knopf, 1956).
10. Alan L. Clem, "The Study of State Politics: Its Purpose, Progress, and Prospects," paper presented at the 25th annual meeting of the Midwest Conference of Political Scientists, Purdue University, Lafayette, Indiana (April 29, 1967), p. 14.
11. Key, *Southern Politics*, p. 307.
12. See, for instance Herbert Jacob, "The Consequences of Malapportionment: A Note of Caution," *Social Forces*, 43 (December 1964), 256–261; David Brady and Douglas Edmonds, "One Man, One Vote—So What?" reprinted from *Trans-Action Magazine* in Andrew Scott and Earle Wallace, eds., *Politics, U.S.A.* (Toronto: Macmillan, 1968), pp. 84–93.
13. Thomas R. Dye, *Politics, Economics, and the Public: Policy Outcomes in the American States* (Chicago: Rand McNally, 1966), p. 293.
14. For a critical analysis of this early research, see Herbert Jacob and Michael Lipsky, "Outputs, Structure, and Power: An Assessment of Changes in the Study of State and Local Politics," *Journal of Politics* (May 1968), pp. 510–538.
15. Richard I. Hofferbert, "Elite Influence in State Policy Formation: A Model for Comparative Inquiry," *Polity*, 2 (Spring 1970), 322.
16. John L. Sullivan, "Political Correlates of Social, Economic, and Religious Diversity in the American States," *Journal of Politics*, 35, No. 1 (February 1973), 70–84.
17. John D. Hutcheson, Jr. and George A. Taylor, "Religious Variables, Political System Characteristics, and Policy Outputs in the American States," *American Journal of Political Science*, 17, No. 2 (May 1973), 414–421.
18. Edward G. Carmines, "The Mediating Influence of State Legislatures on the Linkage Between Interparty Competition and Welfare Policies," *American Political Science Review*, 68, No. 3 (September 1974), 1,118–1,124.
19. Solomon Fabricant, *The Trend of Government Activity in the United States Since 1900* (New York: National Bureau of Economic Research, 1952), pp. 112–139.

20. Ira Sharkansky, *Spending in the American States* (Chicago: Rand McNally, 1968).
21. Thomas J. Anton, *The Politics of State Expenditure in Illinois* (Urbana: University of Illinois Press, 1966), p. 252.
22. Sharkansky, *Spending.*
23. Hofferbert, "Elite Influence," p. 327ff.
24. This is drawn from Sharkansky, *Spending*, pp. 137–138.
25. Virginia Gray, "The Effect of Party Competition on State Policy, a Reformulation: Organizational Survival," *Polity*, 7, No. 2 (Winter 1974), 248–263.
26. See Ira Sharkansky and Richard I. Hofferbert, "Dimensions of State Politics, Economics, and Public Policy," *American Political Science Review*, 63 (September 1969), 867–879, and Charles F. Cnudde and Donald J. McCrone, "Party Competition and Welfare Policies in the American States," *American Political Science Review*, 63 (September 1969), 858–866.
27. Harmon Zeigler and Karl F. Johnson, *The Politics of Education in the States* (Indianapolis, Ind.: Bobbs-Merrill Co., 1972), pp. 73–75.
28. Duane Lockard, "State Party Systems and Policy Outputs," in Oliver Garceau, ed., *Political Research and Political Theory* (Cambridge, Mass.: Harvard University Press, 1968), pp. 190–215.
29. See Friedman, "State Politics," pp. 477–519.
30. R. Fry and Richard F. Winters, "The Politics of Redistribution," *American Political Science Review*, 64, No. 2 (June 1970), 508–522. See also Bernard H. Booms and James R. Halldorson, "The Politics of Redistribution: A Reformulation," *American Political Science Review*, 67, No. 3 (September 1973), 924–933 for a critique of the Fry–Winters methods. However, this more recent analysis still found political factors more significant than economic variables in redistribution policy.
31. Jack L. Walker, "The Diffusion of Innovations Among the American States," *American Political Science Review*, 63 (September 1969), 880–899.
32. Ibid., p. 887.
33. Robert S. Erikson, "The Relationship Between Party Control and Civil Rights Legislation in the American States," *Western Political Quarterly*, 24, No. 1 (March 1971), 178–182.
34. G. Ross Stephens, "State Centralization and the Erosion of Local Autonomy," *Journal of Politics*, 36, No. 1 (February 1974), 44–76.
35. John G. Grumm and Russell D. Murphy, "Dillon's Rule Reconsidered," *The Annals of the American Academy of Political and Social Science*, 416 (November 1974), 120–132.
36. Advisory Commission on Intergovernmental Relations, *Regional Decision-Making: New Strategies for Substate Districts*, vol. 1 (Washington, D.C.: Advisory Commission on Intergovernmental Relations, 1973), chap. 5.
37. Ibid., p. 222.
38. N. Joseph Cayer, *Public Personnel Administration in the United States* (New York: St. Martin's Press, 1975), p. 104.
39. Quoted in Neal Riemer, *James Madison* (New York: Washington Square Press, 1968), p. 141.
40. See Samuel H. Beer, "The Modernization of American Federalism," *Publius*, 3, No. 2 (Fall 1973), 85–87.

Bibliography

The following bibliography offers the reader some possibilities for further reading in American state politics. I have tried to concentrate on general books and articles, those useful in looking at the politics of any state, especially studies to which I did not refer in the text. The materials are arranged according to the main topics of the book.

CHAPTER I

Several books deal generally with the development of the states in the twentieth century. The most comprehensive treatment is W. Brooke Graves, *American State Government*, 4th ed. (Boston: D.C. Heath, 1953). A more succinct text is John C. Buechner, *State Government in the Twentieth Century* (Boston: Houghton Mifflin, 1967). Edward W. Chester investigates various issues in state histories since 1876 in *Issues and Responses in State Political Experience* (Totowa, N.J.: Littlefield, Adams, 1968). A good analysis of the states in the period from 1920 to 1940 is James T. Patterson, *The New Deal and the States* (Princeton, N.J.: Princeton University Press, 1969). Former North Carolina governor Terry Sanford considers trends since the New Deal in *Storm Over the States* (New York: McGraw-Hill, 1967).

Among current appraisals of the states, the most detailed are Neal R. Peirce's several volumes which focus on separate regions of the country. To date these works include *The Megastates of America* (1972), *The Pacific States of America* (1972), *The Mountain States of America* (1971), *The Great Plain States of America* (1973), *The Deep South States of America* (1974), and *The Border South States* (1975). All are published by W. W. Norton and Co., New York, New York. Ira Sharkansky looks in detail at the policy accomplishments of the states in *The Maligned States* (New York: McGraw-Hill, 1972). A treatment of state problems from the point of view of a practitioner, in this case a Connecticut commissioner of environmental protection, is found in Dan W. Lufkin, *Many Sovereign States* (New York: David McKay, 1975).

York Willbern, "States as Components in an Areal Division of Powers," in Arthur Maass (ed.), *Area and Power* (Glencoe, Ill.: The Free Press, 1959), offers an excellent and still relevant theoretical perspective on the states on pages 70–88. The late V. O. Key, Jr., pioneered modern comparative studies of state politics in two books: *Southern Politics in State and Nation* (New York: Knopf, 1949), and *American State Politics: An Introduction* (New York: Knopf, 1956). The best current volume that is consistently comparative in its approach is Herbert Jacob and Kenneth N. Vines (eds.), *Politics in the American States*, 3rd ed. (Boston: Little, Brown, 1976). The application of systems analysis to the ordering of materials on state affairs is exemplified in Robert E. Crew, Jr.'s anthology *State Politics: Readings in Political Behavior* (Belmont, Calif.: Wadsworth, 1968). A more rigorous use of systems analysis in looking at the politics of a single state is Dan Nimmo and William E. Oden, *The Texas Political System* (Englewood Cliffs, N.J.: Prentice-Hall, 1971).

CHAPTER II

A concise overview of federalism in the United States is Richard H. Leach, *American Federalism* (New York: Norton, 1970). Michael D. Reagan criticizes the legal approach to the subject of federalism and argues for a concept of "permissive federalism" in *The New Federalism* (New York: Oxford University Press, 1972). A useful anthology stressing the cooperative nature of American federalism is Daniel J. Elazar, R. Bruce Carroll, E. Lester Levine, and Douglas St. Angelo (eds.), *Cooperation and Conflict* (Itasca, Ill.: Peacock Publishers, 1969). Harry N. Scheiber provides a sharp rebuttal to the sharing thesis of Morton Grodzins and Daniel Elazar in *The Condition of American Federalism: An Historian's View* (Washington, D.C.: U. S. Senate Subcommittee on Intergovernmental Relations, 1966). A volume that discusses some of the group conflicts in federalism is Grant McConnell, *Private Power and American Democracy* (New York: Knopf, 1967). Donald H. Haider, *When Governments Come to Washington* (New York: The Free Press, 1974) explores intergovernmental lobbying in Washington. Paul R. Dommel affords a historical and critical treatment of the emergence of the Revenue Sharing Act of 1972 in *The Politics of Revenue Sharing* (Bloomington, Ind.: Indiana University Press, 1974). Richard P. Nathan, Allen D. Manvel, Susannah E. Calkins, and Associates, *Monitoring Revenue Sharing* (Washington, D.C.: The Brookings Institution, 1975) analyze the use of revenue-sharing dollars in selected states and cities.

Political scientists are paying increasing attention to environmental tensions within the states. The rural-urban conflict has perhaps been treated most extensively. A critical discussion of this literature is provided by Robert S. Friedman, "The Urban-Rural Conflict Revisited," *Western Political Quarterly*,

14 (June 1969), 481–495. Gordon E. Baker has examined rural-urban tensions in relation to state legislative apportionment in two books: *Rural versus Urban Political Power* (New York: Doubleday, 1955), and *The Reapportionment Revolution* (New York: Random House, 1966). Glen T. Broach explores urban-rural conflicts in voting behavior in four state legislatures in "A Comparative Dimensional Analysis of Partisan and Urban-Rural Voting in State Legislatures," *Journal of Politics*, 34, No. 4 (November 1972), 905–921. John H. Fenton examines the problem of sectionalism in four states (Missouri, Kentucky, West Virginia, and Maryland), with emphasis on historic patterns of settlement in these areas, in *Border State Politics* (New Orleans: The Hauser Press, 1957). Raymond E. Wolfinger and Fred I. Greenstein examine a leading contemporary case of state sectionalism, stressing differences in attitude among sectional elites, in "Comparing Political Regions: The Case of California," *American Political Science Review*, 63 (March 1969), 74–85.

An able general discussion of state political cultures that looks at some of the factors associated with variations in culture is Samuel C. Patterson, "The Political Cultures of the American States," *Journal of Politics*, 30 (February 1968) 187–209. Daniel J. Elazar's thesis of political cultures is most fully presented in his *Cities of the Prairie: The Metropolitan Frontier and American Politics* (New York: Basic Books, 1970). A detailed use of the culture concept in the understanding of the politics of an urban state is illustrated in Edgar Litt, *The Political Cultures of Massachusetts* (Cambridge, Mass.: M.I.T. Press, 1965). For an interesting treatment of the impact of culture on the politics of a rural state, see Frank M. Bryan, *Yankee Politics in Rural Vermont* (Hanover, N.H.: University Press of New England, 1974).

CHAPTER III

Two useful introductions to the relationship between public opinion and public policy are V. O. Key, Jr. *Public Opinion and American Democracy* (New York: Knopf, 1961), and Norman R. Luttberg, (ed.), *Public Opinion and Public Policy: Models of Political Linkage* (Homewood, Ill.: The Borsey Press, 1968). A study of attitudes of state electorates in relation to public policy is Ronald E. Weber, *Public Policy Preferences in the States* (Bloomington, Indiana: Institute of Public Administration, 1971). Anne H. Hopkins shows that opinion support needed for policy enactment varies with policy questions in "Opinion Publics and Support for Public Policy in the American States," *American Journal of Political Science*, 18, No. 1 (February 1974), 167–177. Ronald E. Webber and William R. Shaffer, "Public Opinion and American State Policy-Making," *Midwest Journal of Political Science*, 16, No. 4 (November 1972), 683–699 explore the interaction of public opinion, political system characteristics, and state socioeconomic environments and their effect on policy decisions. Robert S. Erikson, "The Relationship between Public Opinion and State Policy: A New Look Based on Some Forgotten Data," *American Journal of Political Science*, 20, No. 1 (February 1976), 25–36 shows that states can be responsive to their constituents on certain "morality" questions.

Several texts on American political parties pay particular attention to state parties. An early and still useful treatment is Austin Ranney and Willmoore Kendall, *Democracy and the American Party System* (New York: Harcourt Brace Jovanovich, 1956), especially chapters 7 and 8. Allan P. Sindler compares American one-party and two-party systems in *Political Parties in the United States* (New York: St. Martin's Press, 1966). An attempt to classify state party systems, with commendable attention to problems of measurement, is Richard I. Hofferbert, "Classification of American State Party Systems," *Journal of Politics*, 26 (August 1964), 550–567. The decomposition of political parties is the theme of much of the work of Walter Dean Burnham. See his "The Changing Shape of the American Political Universe," *American Political Science Review*, 54, No. 1 (March 1965), 7–27; and *Critical Elections and the Mainsprings of American Politics* (New York: Basic Books, 1970). Several excellent treatments of state parties within specific regions of the country are available. Among those not cited elsewhere in this bibliography are Frank H. Jonas (ed.), *Politics in the American West* (Salt Lake City, Utah: University of Utah Press, 1969), John H. Fenton, *Midwest Politics* (New York: Holt, Rinehart, and Winston, 1966), William C. Havard (ed.), *The Changing Politics of the South* (Baton Rouge, La.: Louisiana State University Press, 1972), and Duane Lockard, *New England State Politics* (Princeton, N.J.: Princeton University Press, 1959). Louis M. Seagull traces the rise of the Republican party in the South since 1940 in *Southern Republicanism* (Cambridge, Mass.: Schenkman Publishing Co., 1975). For a discussion of the problems of campaigning in state politics, see Jerome M. Mileur and George T. Sulzner, *Campaigning for the Massachusetts Senate: Electioneering Outside the Political Limelight* (Amherst, Mass.: University of Massachusetts Press, 1974). An important study of electoral behavior in the states is David M. Kovenock, James W. Prothro, and Associates, *Explaining the Vote: Presidential Choices in the Nation and the States, 1968* (Chapel Hill, N.C.: University of North Carolina, Institute for Research in Social Science, 1973).

Harmon Zeigler and Michael Baer have written the best comparative analysis of lobbying and interest group activity in the states in *Lobbying: Interaction and Influence in American State Legislatures* (Belmont, Calif: Wadsworth, 1969). Three good case studies of interest groups in individual states are Frank A. Pinner, Paul Jacobs, and Philip Selznick, *Old Age and Political Behavior* (Berkeley: University of California Press, 1959), which deals with the California Institute of Social Welfare, Andrew Hacker, "Pressure Politics in Pennsylvania: The Truckers vs. the Railroads," in Alan Westin (ed.), *The Uses of Power* (New York: Harcourt Brace Jovanovich, 1962), and James Phelan and Robert Pozen, *The Company State* (New York: Grossman Publishers, 1973), which is concerned with the E. I. Du Pont Company in Delaware. Legislative attitudes toward interest groups are examined in John C. Wahlke, William Buchanan, Heinz Eulau, and Leroy C. Ferguson, "American State Legislators' Role Orientations Toward Pressure Groups," *Journal of Politics*, 22 (February 1960), 203–227.

Albert L. Sturm has prepared two comprehensive surveys of state constitutional changes covering recent decades: *Thirty Years of State Constitution-*

Making, 1938–1968 (New York: National Municipal League, 1970), and *Trends in State Constitution-Making 1966–1972* (Lexington, Ky.: The Council of State Governments, 1973). Most states use constitutional commissions, established by the legislature, as a means of formulating alterations in their basic charters. The politics surrounding the work of one of these agencies is described in detail in William H. Stewart, Jr., *The Alabama Constitutional Commission* (University, Ala: University of Alabama Press, 1975). A group of New England-based scholars has compared the activities of several recently held state constitutional conventions. Elmer E. Cornwell, Jr., Jay S. Goodman, Wayne R. Swanson, "State Constitutional Conventions: Delegates, Roll Calls, and Issues," *Midwest Journal of Political Science*, 14, No. 1 (February 1970), 105–130 examine the relationship between the way delegates to constitutional conventions are chosen and the work they do. For a treatment of the difficulties of securing ratification of convention-prepared constitutional drafts, see Jay S. Goodman, Robert Arseneau, Elmer E. Cornwell, Jr., and Wayne R. Swanson, "Public Responses to State Constitutional Revision," *American Journal of Political Science*, 17, No. 3 (August 1973), 571–596.

CHAPTER IV

An excellent study of state legislative behavior, stressing the various roles played by legislators, is John C. Wahlke, Heinz Eulau, William Buchanan, and Leroy C. Ferguson, *The Legislative System: Explorations in Legislative Behavior* (New York: John Wiley, 1962). The connection between the recruitment of legislators and their activities in one state legislature is systematically examined in Frank J. Sorauf, *Party and Representation: Legislative Politics in Pennsylvania* (New York: Atherton Press, 1963). A comparative treatment of public attitudes toward state legislatures is Samuel C. Patterson, Ronald D. Hedlund, and G. R. Boynton, *Representatives and Represented: Basis of Support for American Legislatures* (New York: Wiley–Interscience, 1975). A good general text comparing state and national legislative institutions is William J. Keefe and Morris S. Ogul, *The American Legislative Process: Congress and the States*, 4th ed. (Englewood Cliffs, N.J.: Prentice-Hall, 1977). Douglas C. Chaffey provides a valuable analysis of legislative institutionalization, focusing on Wisconsin and Montana, in "The Institutionalization of State Legislatures: A Comparative Study," *Western Political Quarterly*, 23, No. 1 (March 1970), 180–196.

The standard work on American governors is Coleman B. Ransone, *The Office of Governor in the United States* (University, Ala.: University of Alabama Press, 1956). For more recent developments in the governorship, see Coleman B. Ransone (ed.), "The American Governor in the 1970's: A Symposium," *Public Administration Review*, 30 (January-February 1970). Joseph A. Schlesinger has examined the political backgrounds of governors in two books: *How They Became Governor: A Study of Comparative State Politics*, 1870–1950 (East Lansing: Michigan State University Governmental Research Bureau,

1957), and *Ambition and Politics: Political Careers in the United States* (Chicago: Rand McNally, 1966). A detailed comparison of the governorship and the presidency is developed in Joseph E. Kallenbach, *The American Chief Executive: The Presidency and the Governorship* (New York: Harper and Row, 1966).

The literature on the long-neglected field of state administration is slowly growing. Thad Beyle and J. Oliver Williams, *The American Governor in Behavioral Perspective* (New York: Harper and Row, 1972) contains several articles on the relationship between the governor and state bureaucrats. A short but well documented survey of state and local administrative problems is Douglas M. Fox, *The Politics of City and State Bureaucracy* (Pacific Palisades, Calif.: Goodyear Publishing Co., 1974). The arrangement and operation of the governors' offices are described in Donald P. Sprengel, *Gubernatorial Staffs: Functional and Political Profiles* (Iowa City: Institute of Public Affairs — University of Iowa, 1969). Alan J. Wyner, "Gubernatorial Relations with Legislators and Administrators," *State Government*, 41, No. 3 (Summer 1968), 199–203 provides a first-hand account of governors' power relationships with other state elites. Thad Beyle, "The Governor's Formal Powers: A View from the Governor's Chair," *Public Administration Review*, 28, No. 4 (November-December 1968), 540–545 analyzes the problem of gubernatorial power according to what governors themselves say about the matter.

A good introductory volume on the politics and problems of state courts is Henry R. Glick and Kenneth N. Vines, *State Court Systems* (Englewood Cliffs, N.J.: Prentice-Hall, Inc., 1973). A detailed analysis of four state supreme courts that stresses judicial roles is Henry R. Glick, *Supreme Courts in State Politics* (Englewood Cliffs, N.J.: Prentice-Hall, Inc., 1971). Suggestions for court reform are contained in Harry W. Jones (ed.), *The Courts, the Public, and the Law Explosion* (Englewood Cliffs, N.J.: Prentice-Hall, 1965). The Missouri plan of judicial selection is examined in depth in Richard A. Watson and Rondal G. Downing, *The Politics of the Bench and the Bar: Judicial Selection Under the Missouri Nonpartisan Court Plan* (New York: John Wiley, 1969). An excellent treatment of the policy-making functions of a trial court is Kenneth M. Dolbeare, *Trial Courts in Urban Politics* (New York: John Wiley, 1967). An important source for comparative research on state courts is *State Court Systems* (Chicago: Council of State Governments, 1974).

CHAPTER V

A succinct introduction to problems of state finances is L. I. Ecker-Racz, *The Politics and Economics of State–Local Finance* (Englewood Cliffs, N.J.: Prentice-Hall, 1970). Ira Sharkansky examines the factors governing differences in state spending in *Spending in the American States* (Chicago: Rand McNally, 1968). A survey of the efforts of the states to modernize their budget practices is Allen Schick, *Budget Innovation in the States* (Washington, D.C.: The Brookings Institution, 1971).

Two important sources on state highway policies are Philip H. Burch, Jr., *Highway Revenue and Expenditure Policy in the United States* (New Brunswick, N.J.: Rutgers University Press, 1962), and Wilfred Owen, *The Metropolitan Transportation Problem* (Washington, D.C.: The Brookings Institution, 1966). A number of valuable case studies are available in the area of state educational policies. See especially Nicholas A. Masters, Robert H. Salisbury, and Thomas H. Eliot, *State Politics and the Public Schools* (New York: Knopf, 1964), Harmon Zeigler and Karl F. Johnson, *The Politics of Education in the States* (Indianapolis, Ind.: Bobbs-Merrill, 1972), and Roald F. Campbell and Tim L. Mazzoni (eds.), *State Policy-Making for the Public Schools: A Comparative Analysis* (Columbus, Ohio: Ohio State University Press, 1974). Two general discussions focusing on the problem of reform of the U. S. welfare system are Gilbert Steiner, *The State of Welfare* (Washington, D.C.: The Brookings Institution, 1971), and Council for Economic Development, *Improving the Public Welfare System* (New York, 1970).

Among the leading studies stressing the importance of economic development in shaping the policies of the states are Richard E. Dawson and James A. Robinson, "Inter-Party Competition, Economic Variables, and Welfare Policies in the American States," *Journal of Politics*, 25, (May 1963), 265–289, and Thomas R. Dye, *Politics, Economics, and the Public: Policy Outcomes in the American States* (Chicago: Rand McNally, 1966). Richard I. Hofferbert "State and Community Policy Studies: A Review of Comparative Input–Output Analysis," *Political Science Annual, Vol. III,* James A. Robinson (ed.), (Indianapolis, Ind.: Bobbs-Merrill, 1972) provides an excellent overview of the state policy literature. The willingness of states to innovate in various policy areas has received considerable attention in the 1970s. See especially Virginia Gray, "Innovations in the States: A Diffusion Study," *American Political Science Review,* 67, No. 4 (December 1973), 1,174–1,185, and *Innovations in State Government* (Washington, D.C.: National Governors' Conference, 1974). A somewhat different approach to redistribution policies from that in the text is Richard DeLeon, "Politics, Economics, and Redistribution in the American States: A Test of a Theory," *American Journal of Political Science,* 17, No. 4 (November 1973), 781–796.

The federal impact on state public policies is analyzed in James C. Strouse and Philippe Jones, "Federal Aid: The Forgotten Variable in State Policy Research," *Journal of Politics*, 36, No. 1 (February 1974), 200–207. The general problem of the states in the intergovernmental system has recently been the topic of an entire issue of two journals: see "The Federal Polity," *Publius*, 3, No. 2 (Fall 1973), and "Intergovernmental Relations in America Today," *Annals of the American Academy of Social and Political Science*, 416 (November 1974). An insightful introductory volume on intergovernmental relations is Daniel J. Elazar, *American Federalism: A View from the States*, 2nd ed. (New York: T. Y. Crowell, 1972).

Index

Activists, 12, 14, 62
"Advertisers," 92
AFL-CIO, 78, 79
Alabama, 68, 77
Alaska, 51
American Institute of Public
    Opinion, 59
A-95 review power, 141

Back to Thirteen States (Brown), 38
Baker v. *Carr*, 1, 15, 41, 95, 128
Barber, James, 91
Birth, A. H., 59
Brown, John Stafford, 38
Brown v. *Board of Education*, 113
Bureaucracy, 100
   and political culture, 46, 47, 48
Byrd, Harry F., 69

Calhoun, John C., 28
California, 10, 35, 43, 70, 82, 96,
    114, 115, 125, 126
Cameron, Simon, 69
Carmines, Edward, 132
Caucus, 93, 94
Cities. *See* Urban centers
Civil Rights Act of 1964, 30, 34
Civil rights legislation, 30, 34,
    60, 137

Cohens v. *Virginia*, 27
Colorado, 140
Combs, Bert, 134
Common Cause, 80
Community Development Act of
    1974, 141
Conservation, 84, 136
Constitutional amendments, 81, 84
Constitutional Convention, 24
Construction Construed and Con-
    stitutions Vindicated
    (Taylor), 28
Cotter, Cornelius, 62
Crump, Edward, 13

Delaware, 76
Dolbeare, Kenneth, 110
Dual federalism, 29, 30, 31
Dye, Thomas, 129, 130, 133

Education, 25, 113 – 114, 120,
    122 – 123, 125, 135, 136
E. I. Du Pont Company, 76
Elazar, Daniel, 45, 47, 48, 49
Electoral college, 33
Environmental issues, 84, 140, 141
Ethnic diversity
   and political culture, 47 – 48
   and state politics, 53

Executive leadership, 97, 98 – 99, 101, 105. *See also* State executive

Expenditures. *See* State budgets

Federal government, 25, 82
  and aid to states, 36 – 37, 120, 121
  and constitutional politics, 81, 82
  and political system, 19
  and public welfare, 123 – 124
  and state growth, 4
  and state political reorganization, 15 – 16
  as regulating body, 33
  functions of, 8
  state involvement with, 141 – 143
  and state political visibility, 7 – 9, 11

Federalism, 2
  conflicts concerning, 25 – 31
  defined, 24
  dual, 29, 30, 31
  functional, 36 – 37
  politics of, 31 – 39

Fenton, John, 70, 71
Ferguson, Jim "Pa," 68
Ferguson, Miriam "Ma," 68
Fiscal Assistance Act, 37
Florida, 10, 16, 43, 140
Folsom, "Kissin'" Jim, 68
Functional federalism, 36 – 37

Governmental Process, The (Truman), 32
Governors. *See* State executive
"Granger laws," 34
Grants-in-aid, 7 – 8, 9, 36, 37, 100, 120, 121, 122, 124
Grodzins, Morton, 25
Gunther, John, 44

Hamilton, Alexander, 26, 28
Hammer v. *Dagenhart,* 29
Hennessy, Bernard, 62
Highway programs, 121, 124, 125, 135

Idaho, 43, 61
Illinois, 70, 71, 72
Income tax, 121, 122, 140
Incrementalism, 133, 134
Independents (political party), 73, 74
Indiana, 39, 40, 70, 71, 72
Inside U.S.A. (Gunther), 44
Institutionalization, 100
  and court system, 110
  causes of, 94 – 95
  in state legislatures, 91 – 93
  in U.S. House of Representatives, 89 – 90
Interest groups, 32 – 39, 58, 99, 100
  and political parties, 74, 79
  and "public interest," 80
  and state constitutions, 82, 83 – 84
  state-national comparisons of, 75 – 78
Intergovernmental Personnel Act (IPA) of 1970, 142
Interstate Commerce Commission, 34
Iowa, 40

Jackson, Andrew, 29
Jefferson, Thomas, 28
Johnson, Lyndon B., 36
Judicial Qualification Commission, 115

Kaufman, Herbert, 97
Kentucky, 69, 134
Key, V. O., Jr., 14, 68, 73, 127, 128
Kingdon, John, 77

La Follette, Robert, 34
Lasswell, Harold, 17
Leadership committee, 94
Legislative compensation, 95, 96
Legislative reapportionment, 1, 4, 16, 39, 80, 83, 95, 96
Lindsay, John, 43

Lobbying, 74, 75, 78. *See also*
  Interest groups
Local government, 82, 84, 133
  and interest groups, 80
  and public welfare, 124
  and state centralization, 139 –141
  and state growth, 5 – 6
  fragmentation of, 13
  functions of, 8
Long, Huey, 69
Louisiana, 5, 69
Lowden, Frank, 98

McConnell, Grant, 77
McCulloch v. *Maryland,* 27, 28
Madison, James, 142
Magazines and journals, 11, 12
Main, Jackson Turner, 40
Maine, 70, 80, 114
Marbury v. *Madison,* 26
Marchetti v. *United States,* 30
Marshall, John, 26, 27, 29, 30
Maryland, 39, 61, 84, 140
Massachusetts, 5, 10, 43
Mass media, 11, 12, 72, 73
Mencken, H. L., 39
Michigan, 71, 92
Minnesota, 71
Mississippi, 44, 51, 121
Missouri, 13
Munger, Frank, 59, 60
Municipal government. *See* Local
  government
Muskie, Edmund, 33, 70

Nader, Ralph, 76
National government. *See* Federal
  government
Nebraska, 43
Neutral competence, 97, 98, 99,
  101
New Deal, 29
"New Federalism," 2, 11, 37
New Jersey, 11, 44
Newspapers, 9, 10, 11
New York, 5, 35, 61, 83, 125, 126

O'Daniel, "Pappy," 44

Ohio, 10, 70, 71, 72
Oklahoma, 83
One-party systems, 65, 66, 79, 101
  and public policy, 128, 129
  types of, 68 – 70
  See also Political parties;
    State politics; Two-party
    systems

Pendergast, Tom, 13
Penrose, Boies "Big Grizzly," 69
"Petty" courts, 108, 114
Plunkitt, George Washington, 43
Political culture
  and interparty competition, 65
  and public policy, 131, 132
  types of, 45 – 49
Political machines, 13, 97
Political organizations, 13, 18,
  49. *See also* Political parties
Political participation, and political
  culture, 46, 47, 49
Political parties, 18, 49, 58,
  101, 132
  and interparty competition,
    63 – 66
  and public policy, 177, 178
  decentralization of, 63, 67
  organization of, 62
  problems of, 73 – 74
  responsibility of, 72
  varieties of, 68 – 72
  See also Interest groups; One-
    party systems; Political or-
    ganizations; State politics;
    Two-party systems
Political system, 18 – 20, 75
  and public policy, 130, 131, 138
Political visibility, 7 – 12, 40
Politics, Economics, and the Public
  (Dye), 129, 130, 133
Polsby, Nelson, 89, 94
Populist party, 41
Property tax, 140
Public administration. *See* State
  administration
Public employment, 4, 5 – 6
"Public Interest" lobby, 80

Public opinion, 58
  and public policy, 59 – 62
Public policy (state)
  and federalism, 139 – 143
  and interest groups, 33, 78
  and judiciary, 109, 113 – 114
  and party responsibility, 71, 72
  and party structure, 67, 69, 70, 71
  and political culture, 46, 47, 49
  and political visibility, 10
  and public opinion, 59 – 62
  and reapportionment, 96
  and state executive, 104 – 105
  expenditures for, 51, 53, 122 – 126
  factors affecting, 127 – 139
  political system and, 18
questions of, 126
  revenues for, 120 – 122
  types of, 119
Public welfare, 46, 71, 120, 123 – 124, 125, 129, 132, 135, 136

Quay, Matthew, 69

Ranney, Austin, 64, 65
Reagan, Ronald, 104
Reapportionment. *See* Legislative reapportionment
"Reluctants," 92, 95
Representativeness, 97 – 98, 99, 101
Revenue. *See* State budgets
Revenue sharing, 2, 3, 6, 37, 100 120
Rockefeller, Nelson, 104
Roosevelt, Franklin, 33
Roosevelt, Theodore, 34
Rosenthal, Alan, 93
Rural-urban tensions, 39, 40, 41 111, 112

Sales tax, 121, 122, 140
Sanford, Terry, 102

Schlesinger, Joseph A., 101
Sectionalism, 42 – 45
Seniority system, 90, 92
Separation of powers, 73
Serrano v. *Priest*, 114
Sharkansky, Ira, 133
Sorauf, Frank, 74
South Dakota, 9
Southern Politics in State and Nation (Key), 14
Spending, 4, 5, 10, 11, 48, 96, 105, 120
  changes in, 133 – 135
  See also State budgets
Squirearchy, 14 – 15
Standard Metropolitan Statistical Areas (SMSAs), 39
Standing committees, 90, 92 93 – 94, 96
State administration, 33, 125
  improvements in, 105 – 107
  problems of, 97 – 105
  See also Activists; State executive
State budgets, 103, 105, 106, 120 – 126, 142
  expenditures, 78, 96, 122 – 126, 128, 129, 132, 136
  factors affecting, 132 – 135
  revenues, 96, 120, 121, 122, 140
  See also Grants-in-aid; Public policy; Revenue sharing; Spending
State capital, 9, 10
State constitutions
  and U.S. Constitution, 81 – 82
  "majoritarian" aspect of, 81
  politics of, 80, 82 – 84
  See also State politics; U.S. Constitution
State courts, 83, 111
  and public policy, 113 – 114
  politics of, 109 – 113
  reforms in, 114 – 115
  structure of, 107 – 109
  See also "Petty" courts; Trial courts

State executive, 15, 16, 83, 95, 97
  and policy-making process,
    102 – 103
  political advantages of,
    103 – 104
  powers of, 98 – 99, 101 – 102,
    105 – 107
  restrictions upon, 99 – 100
State government
  and federal government, 142, 143
  and interest groups, 77 – 79
  and political parties, 64 – 66,
    67 – 71, 74
  and political system, 18 – 19
  and public policy, 59 – 60
  and rural-urban tensions, 39,
    40, 41
  and state constitutions, 82, 83, 84
  as regulating body, 32, 33
  budgets for, 120 – 126, 133 – 135
  centralization of, 139 – 141
  conduct of, 92 – 94
  criticism of, 2 – 3, 6, 10
  fragmentation of, 13
  functions of, 8 – 9
  governing coalitions in, 12,
    14 – 16
  growth of, 4, 5
  problems of, 7 – 16, 99
State legislative district, 76
State legislatures, 1, 15, 16, 39,
    41, 48, 83, 88 – 97
  and administrative changes, 107
  and institutionalization, 89, 93,
    94, 95
  and interest groups, 78
  and interparty competition, 66
  and personnel turnover rate,
    91 – 92
  and public policy, 127, 132
  and state executive, 100, 103, 104
  ambiguity of, 88 – 89
  compared to U.S. Congress, 91,
    92, 94, 96
  conflicts in, 45
  reform of, 95 – 97

State politics
  and communication problems,
    9 – 10, 11
  and federalism, 24 – 30
  and idea of power, 17, 18
  and interest groups, 31 – 39,
    74 – 80
  and public opinion, 59 – 62
  and public policy, 120, 126 – 138
  and state constitutions, 80 – 84
  and state courts, 109 – 113
  and state executive, 98 – 100,
    102 – 105
  and state legislatures, 88 – 96
  attitudes toward, 39 – 55
  cohesiveness of, 44 – 45
  defined, 17
  differences in, 49 – 54
  political organizations in, 13 – 14
  political parties in, 62 – 74
  public interest in, 1 – 2, 38
  sectionalism and, 42 – 43
  See also Interest groups; Political
    organizations; Political parties
State rights position, 28 – 29, 31,
    32, 35
Stone, Harlan, 30
Subnational governments. *See* Local
    government; State government
Systems model, 19 – 20, 88
  See also Political system

Talmadge, Gene "Wild Man from
    Sugar Creek," 68
Taney, Roger B., 29
Taylor, John, 28, 29
Taxation, 83, 105, 140
  and public policy, 10, 11,
    121 – 122
  See also Public policy; State
    budgets
Television. *See* Mass media
Tennessee, 13
Tenth Amendment, 29, 30
Texas, 64, 68, 114
Tocqueville, Alexis de, 42

Transfer payments, 5
Trial courts, 108, 109, 110
Truman, David, 31, 32, 75
Two-party systems, 64, 65, 66, 67,
    79, 80, 135
  and public policy, 128, 129
  types of, 70 – 72
  See also One-party systems;
    Political parties; State politics

Urban centers, 6, 49
  state concern with, 40 – 42
  See also Local government
U.S. Congress, 91, 92
U.S. Constitution, 25, 26, 27, 28,
    81, 82, 83
U.S. Supreme Court, 1, 15, 34, 39,
    81, 82, 83, 113

and Federalism, 25 – 31
Utah, 41

Vermont, 140
Virginia, 69

Walker, Jack, 137
Wallace, George, 69
Weber, Max, 62
West Virginia, 11
Wilson, Woodrow, 34
Wisconsin, 71, 77, 121
Wyoming, 76
Wyoming Stock Growers
    Association, 76

Zeller, Belle, 79, 80, 83